CONTENTS

SPECIAL THANKS

Special thanks to all the Jones Family who I love so dearly. Special thanks to my sisters and brothers.

I want to thank:
Brenda Jones
Sherline Jones
Bobby Jones
Benjamin Jones
Anita Jones
Warren Jones

I like to thank the precious part of my family that has gone on to be with the Lord.

Rena Jones
Flornette Jones
Most of all I want to thank my mother the leader and the strength of this family Mrs. Leora Jones

Special Thanks to Minister Gloria Jones who first gave me the Gospel with love. God Bless the Jones Family we are all blessed.

SPECIAL THANKS

I just want to thank my dear friends who help inspire me to write this book. I like to thank my good friends who allowed me the grace to depended on them while going thru a disastrous period in my life. I like to thank those as follow.

Evangelist Elizabeth Johnson
Eugene Wallace
Elder William Rochford
Minister Dale Green
Rachael Green
Pastor Alvin Moses
Missionary Irene Moses
Evangelist Ronnice
And the Congregation of Deliverance Christian Center.

I want to thank this list of noted people for being a great help in my life. For with great friends great things can be accomplished. So I say thank you a million times over. I pray God continue to bless each and every one of you beyond your wildest dream. May he take you to places that you can only imagine, for I know he so desire to do just that. I love each and every one of you with all my heart and soul. I'm so very happy that we meet with each other on this side of heaven.
I consider you as friends and truly a blessing in my life. Thank you for bringing me joy when I needed it.

God Bless You.

INTRODUCTION

You know many of us want God's blessing but don't qualify to receive them. We don't qualify because we haven't been taught by the Holy Spirit to receive them. We don't understand the level of faith it takes to tap into the blessings of God. We sometimes think God should bless us when we haven't been elevated spiritually to the level of maintaining that which we are asking him for. There is a process to receiving God's blessings and this process is set in place by God. We must learn the principles of God before we are spiritually able to receive and maintain what we so desire from him.

The process is methodical and tedious because God is a God of excellence. But we can be assured once we' have gone thru this process we'll be spiritually equipped to receive and maintain any blessing God will bestow upon us. God in this process teaches us systematically how to wait on him and when to move, in so many words we learn perseverance and God's divine timing. The Bible states that when you hear the voice of the Lord we should immediately do that which we have heard. This teaching is essential to the successful people of God who expect to receive from him.

We must come to believe God for who he is and believe him for what he said he would do. What we believe about God will determine what we shall receive from him. If we believe we will surely receive because God word promises this to be so. But in my Christian walk with God I come to know that at crucial times when he's molding his will into our lives we forget there is a process in which we receive from him. We forget because God's molding is painful but truly necessary. The pain which is inflicted upon us is tremendous and hard to bear at times. But when we succumb to the pain of this process we begin to doubt God's love for us. Doubt is the culprit that will stop us from receiving from God. Not receiving from God encourages us to work independently of God and when we work independently of God we soon find ourselves in deep water. Walking independently of God will allow the enemy to produce strongholds in our lives. In turn this steals our joy which is our strength and without strength we become ineffective in God's kingdom. If we're going to receive from God we need to know how to handle the pain of becoming mature. How many know that the joy of the Lord is our strength. But when our joy is gone we are laid open for the enemy for destruction.

So I just want to say the process that I have written in this book is scriptural it shall enlighten you in ways that will strengthen your faith and increase your joy in the Lord. We want the word of God to encourage us, to lift us up and to give strength when we find ourselves weak as we go thru the trails of our lives. I don't come as someone who has all the answers but I come with what the Holy Ghost has inspired me to give to those who will read this book. I am just the messenger of God and I want to make this completely clear. We all struggle with the word at times, and for someone to say they have never struggled with the word is surely a liar and the truth isn't in them.

Even the great people of the bible struggled with the word at times. Some of the old patriarchs question God about situations concerning their lives. But the fact still remained that they all had one thing in common and that common thing was that they had faith that God would do whatever he said he would do. They knew God would give whatever he promised. Each individual were confident that God was faithful to keep his word; they knew he would never deviate from it. So we should be confident of this very thing that whatsoever we ask we shall receive only if we believe, if we believe all things are possible.

SHOUT WITH A PRAISE

PREFACE

Pain and the revelation of God revealed the contents of this book. God out of all my troubles and disobedience gave me grace and a mighty hope in him. He gave me the power to stand and write the principals of this book. By suffering thru he showed me how to apply the principals of maturing and receiving. The principals are common principles that most people have knowledge of. But thou we have knowledge many do not live by them. Without these essential principals instituted in our lives we shall continue to live a life of mediocrity. Most if they were really truthful would tell you they don't have a clue about receiving from God. But many have come to know the way I have come to know and that's thru pain. I strongly believe that when the pain get severe enough from not reaping the things that you desire, when you get so tired of the Devil manipulating and

taking from you, you will desperately find the revelation in God to apply these principals. God is God he will not have you ignorant. He will not stand by and let you continue to fail. Give your heart to God and let him show you the wonderful world of freedom and reaping. He will give you your heart desires, but first we must come to the end of ourselves and at our end is where God begins. When God takes over you can be sure that you will receive whatsoever you ask for.

Have you had enough pain yet? Well if you have then start running after God like you never ran before and watch him do it. Get ready for your miracle.

GOD BLESS YOU AND DREAM LIKE YOU NEVER DREAMED BEFORE IN GOD.

Who Said You Can' Have It.
Chapter One.
God's Spoken Word

First I like to point out that we are God's children and we have the heart of God. Because we have the heart of God we have his love, attention, care and guidance. God is love; God is love in every aspect of the word. For God's creative nature is love. Out of love God created creation not simply for himself but he created creation to share in all the great things he has made. God could have created creation to function like a lifeless robot. He could have created man and beast to obey his every command.

God could have been indescribably selfish and made all that have breath live like emotionless creatures that neither felt nor experienced the five senses of life such as smell, hear touch, see etc. God could have created an assembly line that manufactured man and beast and once taken from the assembly line he could have choose to put into creation a controlling chip that controlled creation every move. But Gods love went beyond any selfish desire. God out of his love allowed the love in him to move past any selfishness. By moving past an unselfish state God allowed creation to experience on a spiritual and emotional plane. So that in a life time man and beast may experience life on a higher plane of life rather than live as an inanimate object that is controlled by him. For it was God's desire that we experienced the fullness of all his creation. He wanted man and beast to experience what love is and the attracting powers of love. So instead of manufacturing man from a hard cold lifeless assembly line, he inserted his spirit in man and imparted in man his nature which was love. Love is the nature of God it's also the nature of man because man is a part of God. So when God created man he formed him from a lifeless amount of clay and inserted in the clay life. He desired man to acknowledge the source in which life is experienced and manipulated. He wanted man to experience the essence of life apart from the clay crafted body.

He wanted man to experience the nature of the essence in which called him to be a living being. God is the essence who is an all loving and understanding God. The essence of life is love and love is what continuously creates man's life until he returns back to the ground. This is the love connection that God so desire for man. He desired that every man and woman should come to understand that he is the essence in which we have our being. Our being is knitted to the acknowledgement that God is the creator and the source of life that gave birth to everything that we see and imagine. He wanted to make clear that all things were created from love because he is love.

Because of love God created purpose for creation; he knew creation needed purpose in order to draw from him. He knew that the inanimate world needed purpose so it would obediently obey the will for its life. The universe has purpose and its full purpose is only known by God. We watch and scientifically chart the movement of the universe so we can somehow come to understand the purpose and the reason for its existence. Our father God knows every assigned work of the universe and knows that all that has been given to the universe will be done perfectly. Our God intently monitor his works to make sure that all that he wills in the inanimate world will be accomplished. God has never been wrong about anything nor will ever be accused of his word failing.

Isaiah 55 states that God word goes out and accomplishes all that it has been set forth to do. Our father isn't a God that occasionally makes mistakes; he isn't a God that fails in managing the things that exist on this side of heaven. He isn't a God that someone has to continuously examine his movements. But God is a perfect God and he's perfect in all his undertaking, he is perfect in all his thoughts. He is perfect in his judgments he applies to our lives. He is forever perfect in positioning purpose, whether it's purpose for the inanimate world or in the lives of his greatest creation which is man. Who has the right and the power to ordain and foresee purpose in our lives but God? He has given birth to all creation. He knows and understands the beginning to the end of everything that exists. God is a God that understands the life span of all creation. Even thou he does not control man in a robotic fashion, he yet do know the very time and date of each birth and each death that will occur. So if God has this information concerning every living creature, then it should be safe to say that God created you out of love and purpose. It should be safe to say that he created you for a specific reason and task in this life time. God knowing all things set dates and times for your birth and for your death.

He set time for your in between laughter and sorrow. He also set dates and times for your reaping and harvesting seasons in your life. God is love and your purpose in life is what keeps him intimately involved with you. What I'm saying is that God is the driving force that keep shaping and forming until you become what he has ordained you to be. Gen: 2:7 explains that God created man and inserted in him himself which was life. If he inserted himself into man, this only mean he inserted love and purpose into man which is his character, and if God is great then God has intended greatness and purpose for your life. Not only has he intended it, his nature and character automatically seals you as someone that is great. You are great and wonderfully made and filled with purpose simply because all that is in God was placed in you by God. What greater nature, what greater love, what greater purpose can be set for your life when God has breathed in you life and his nature and character. God has shaped you for greatness, something greater than you can ever imagine. He has purposed in you a calling that can only be described as fantastically wonderful. He has carved out for you a time here in your life that is so awesome. A call and purpose that is so great that at times when you meditate on it the joy of it will take your breath away. There are no words that can explain his intimate touch and directing in your life.

The experiencing of this personal leading in our lives is most exhilarating even in our bad times. Bad times have taught you that God is the creator and the great director of your life. You come to know by revelation that God knows everything about your present life and future. You depend on his undeniable leadership and his great love that he has for you. You come to know he will bring you out of any situation. In time you came to know his authentic moving in your life. You humbly allowed his intervening which taught you to endure all that would invade your life. But you allowed knowing with confidence that our God will suddenly change our dark times into morning.

.

Psalms: 30:5 Weeping may endure for a night but joy comes in the morning. Joy does comes in the morning to wipe away our tears and fear. Joy demolishes the gray disfigured clouds in our lives. Our joy reminds us that God is on the throne and because we know that he's on the throne we can be sure that nothing will overtake us. We allow God to orchestrate our lives because we have come to witness his power. We understand his power is unmatchable, we also know that God's power will suddenly change the complexity of our situations. In other words God will come thru in an unmistakably way. He will shake our situation and obliterate the sting and hurt of them and replace the damaging pain with peace and joy. God is our problem solver when occasional troublesome situation invade our lives.

God literally subside the emotional attachment that is attached to the situation and allows us to recognize that he is in charge and has everything in control. We thank God for the hard times, because from them we have instinctually learned to let go and let God. In turbulent times we came to know God's love and his greatness and his determination to reveal himself to us. In hard times we come to know his faithfulness and the power of his might to bring us out. We come to know that God is who he says he is. He is our Jehovah Jireh our provider who provides us with every imaginable thing we will possibly ever need. His awesomeness is completely mindboggling and no less than magnificent.

How can we not be overwhelmed by his unprecedented aggressiveness to reveal himself to us? How is it that such a great magnificent God would ever desire to reveal himself to us? How is it that he convincingly invades our lives in regards to show his love and his desire to be our God? His desire for us in our short time we will live on this side of heaven is that we come to know his goodness not only exist in our good times but even more abundantly in our bad times. Our bad times are the breathing grounds where God reveals himself in our troubles and with a strong hand.

Thou we sometimes can barely recognize his presence nor understand some of the devastating situation we find ourselves in, we yet understand that he is bringing us thru. We understand that ever so slowly he is dismantling the weapon that's been formed against us. We understand he is leading us into an expectant end, an end that will reveal the fruits of peace and the mercy of God's fingerprints on our deliverance. This is how we come to know God and his love. We come to know him in our devastating times. We see his fingerprints time after time in our deliverance and so our love grows deeper. Finally we came to depend on his love and care. We utterly realize that his love is all we need in our lives and so we seek to please him and to yield our lives unrestrictedly to his will. We please him because of our concrete knowing that whatever we imagine and whatever we can possibly ever do in our lives we come to know that only God can give us the power to do it or think it. We think on God and commune with him so we can come to know his mind and his thoughts sort of speak. We seek him daily so we may come to know his heart for our lives. As we pursue purpose we also pursue his mind and thoughts which holds a word for our lives. God's spoken word for our lives brings alive the purpose he has ordained in our lives.

His spoken word for your life is the breath that awakens purpose in your life. God's word is the fuel that puts purpose in motion. God's spoken word specifies the specific task that purpose is called to accomplish. His spoken word gives purpose its direction and aim in his kingdom. When purpose is accomplished it ties into God's ultimate plan of salvation for man. What has God spoken in your life that you need to give heed to so that you may accomplish that space or thing that will ultimately help bring man to salvation? What great thing has he whispered into your spirit that you may know without doubt that it was God alone who whispered it?

What is the magnitude of it? How great and awesome is the scope of your purpose? Does it astound you? Does it leave you in awe? Has God whispered awesome wonders to you? Well it wouldn't be God if it wasn't something very awesome. It wouldn't be God if it wasn't completely breathtaking when you thought about it. It wouldn't be God if sometimes you found it hard to believe that God would trust you with such a thing. He is awesome and he believes that you are awesome in everyway simply because he knows that you trust him totally without doubt. He knows you will accomplish everything that he has revealed to you and insurmountably much more.

Who is it that created the heavens and the earth and all living things but our awesome God who is all powerful, all knowing, who is present everywhere. Because he is so awesome he sits in every square inch of the universe. He's so awesome that time evolve at his thought. Is there anyone greater is there anything more powerful and more loving than God. No there is no one like God or anything that comes close to his statues. He is perfect in everyway you can imagine. God desire us to acknowledge him in this way. So therefore he will always without doubt without major concern accomplish the very thing that his word promises to do. He will not let his word go out without prospering in all the ways that he has called for it to do. God does not have Alzheimer nor is he slothful.

Whatever word he has whispered to you about your purpose be assured that he will accomplish it in a clear convincing fashion. So don't become disenchanted if his word hasn't yet been completely performed in your life. Don't be dominated by the things that surround you daily, nor be negatively hypnotized by the circumstances that you encounter. Don't let anything diminish your expectations of God. It frustrates you severely when we take our eyes off God especially when God is bringing alive purpose in our lives. The Word of God gives life to purpose it also centers you right in the middle of your call for your life. There is nothing like resting in the center of God's call on your life. At the center of God's calling on your life is joy unspeakable, peace indescribably, power without measure, love enjoyed immensely.

This is what God word accomplishes when you are placed in the center of your calling; you are fulfilled immeasurably and wholeheartedly. God desire you to abound in his word every awakening moment of your life. He wants you to mediate on it and become consumed by the life of it. He wants us to experience the confidence that his word holds, the faith that it generates, and the power that it display in great difficult times. God's word masterfully presents itself unmistakably great. The word of God does great things in people lives. People like TD Jakes, Benny Hinn, Billy Graham and countless others who God has propelled by his word to extreme heights. I'm pretty sure that the people I just mention had no idea that they would ever be experiencing God in this magnitude in which they are now experiencing him.

Look at Katherine Kullman, the healer who came before Benny Hinn. She was truly a great woman of God who had the evidence of God's power. Katherine Kullman had a healing ministry that was awesome. God used this mighty woman to heal and deliver many of his children in the witness of crowds of people. This great woman of God was truly an awesome woman of God. So if God can change these ordinary people lives into something spectacular and nothing no less than powerful, then God can and will transform your life as well. He gives special attention, special consistency, special molding into your preparation.

Why so special in his molding? Because he is a God of perfection and if we are going to be anything like God well then he has to be very selective on how he molds us. He wants the world to marvel at his creation, he wants the world to be so amazed with us, that when they look upon us they are immediately mesmerized by our beauty and strength. Not the physical beauty, but the bible does state that the righteous shall be beautified by salvation. But what I'm speaking about is the beauty displayed as the world watches you go thru your trails and you yet still somehow have the strength to help others. There is so much to be said about the unyielding spirit that is placed into you by God. Your unwillingness to yield gives testimony to the spirit of God that lives in you. It reveals the strength of God and the power to change minds and hearts as the spirit is revealed.

Is God not awesome? I come to know that he is because he has set his mark on this world. His mark is his word and his word convincing and authentically holds all things together. God and him alone in his triune fashion keeps us and hold us up as he yet holds everything in place.

So his word is the spiritual gas that gives life to your purpose. His word reveals your purpose in life it also gives you the strength to accomplish it here on earth. This is why it is so important that we draw from God's word. When we draw from the power of God's word it strengthens our confidence in God, God's word has revealing factors about our destiny. In God's word lies the seed of revelation for our lives. When revelation has been exposed and imparted into our lives it becomes a part of us or should I say its experience gives us deeper revelation of God. The deeper the experience the easier it is to follow God's instruction for our lives. Our experience in him reveals his love and it helps us with our anticipation for his move in our lives. Our experience in him gives meaning to being solid as a rock. It is definitely easier to have confidence in someone that is powerful and has your best interest in mind. It's easier to hold on when you know that someone is working out the situations that appear in your life. Because when life shows you something other than peace and joy well then the revealed word of God that was whispered to you will shows you how purpose is more important than your situations.

It teaches us to look at the big picture and not just the immediate camera shot of our lives. The revelation of the word shows us how our purpose desperately needs to be fulfilled. I mention in the book earlier that our purpose is interconnected to many people and many spiritual facets that will accomplish certain complexities that God has ordained to be fulfilled. We are purposed to bring people into the saving knowledge of Jesus Christ which is man's salvation. Jesus is the Tree of Salvation, he is the tree of life, and we are the vines or the spiritual limbs of the tree. We all work as one body to accomplish the will of God. So it is very important or imperative that we accomplish all that God has given us to do. Our interconnection holds the plan of God. This is why we can't be slack or slothful about the things of God. We all play a key part in accomplishing God's will. Our obedience and spiritual motivation plays a big part in God's plan. So I believe we should be energized enough to labor with God in his unique plan for man's salvation and for our own joy in God.

Because the joy of the lord is our strength, it is our desire to have strength in God so we can endure the race that is before us. We desire to run the race with patience and faith. We give God the reins of our lives so he can produce that which is needed for us to endure until all things has been revealed. So let us continually to be nourished by our Lord as he sustains us as being part of the tree. Let the whispered word for your life be the imparted spiritual strength that will bring forth the desired results that God has purposed in you. Let the love of God drive you delightfully and boldly to achieving purpose in your life on this side of heaven.

Let his word and purpose continue to consume and overtake us with enough spiritual aggressiveness to defeat the situations and the Devil that tries to invade our life. Let us wait on God in all that we do so that when we move we can move out with confidence as God instruct us. Let us continue to acknowledge God as being our father and the love of our lives. He is more than able to bring us to our knees with awe and reverence. He is more than able to love us with the love of a father and he's surely able to keep us safe. God will be there in our pain and suffering, he will be there when we occasionally lose our way. The bible says that God leaves the 99 sheep and he goes searching for the one sheep that has wandered away. This is how God love is towards us, he will not suffer his children to be lost he will be like a father and come. He will breathe a fresh revelation of our calling into

our lives. So let the love of God and his word and purpose in your life drive you to unusual heights. Let it give you a joy that is unspeakable and unexplainable. And finally let God use you without measure so you can become unmovable in his sight and in the sight of the people that surrounds you.

You are awesome not because you are awesome in yourself and have the power to manifest yourself into any of these words that I just mention. But it is all because he is wonderful and has called you with a great call and purpose for your life. Surely he will give you the power to accomplish that which he has ordained and entrusted you with.

So Lets Just Give Him Praise.

Chapter Two
Desire

Out of purpose desire is born, this desire is born out of thankfulness and love for our God who have saved us and entrusted us with such a great calling. This desire is born from a place of desiring to bring forth purpose in one's life. Godly desires are desires that come about when man is educated by God concerning his purpose. The Holy Spirit begins to reveal in man the necessary instruments that he needs to bring purpose forth. He sometimes reveals this revelation by visions, people, things etc, but however he reveals desires is born. Because our desire comes from God we find ourselves spiritually energized to accomplish the task that is set before us. We are injected with the love and hope of uplifting God's kingdom and marveled by the fact that God is using us to do it. God's desire to use us intensifies our hope of becoming who God called us to be.

Why do our desires intensify? Simply because God is pure and many of us haven't experienced pure things in our lives. We have experienced harmful things that wish our destruction. We have experienced people that desire to destroy us. Some desire to make us as insignificant as a fly on the wall. They corner us in and use us for all that we have and then at the drop of a hat they discard us in desolate places, such as hopelessness, shamefulness, depression and many other places that does not give credibility to the awesomeness of what God have created us for. People will desire to have you unproductive to the point of you depending on them.

Some people just don't feel good unless they feel like they have a little bit more than you. There wish is that you will always need them to help you in some way. People pride will not allow you to gracefully exceed to the point of becoming greater than them. They don't want you to find the ultimate peace because they are not peaceful people. They don't want you to find hope because they are hopeless people. They don't want you to find God because they don't believe in God. I come to find out that the statement misery loves company is so true. People are so miserable in their lives and because they're miserable they desire others to feel the same way. What an awful approach to life and what a negative example of being your brother's keeper.

The greed of humanity is at astronomical proportions, not just with money alone, but with everything that we humanly experience. Society today has a tremendous greed to witness violence. It doesn't matter whether the violence is coming in over our television airways or from the violent video games we purchase from game outlets. Not to mention the violence that is witnessed on the internet. Violence today is truly a problem amongst the masses, especially in undeveloped countries where dictators rule rather than organized government. But even where there's organized government there is still the monster called corruption. The fallout of corruption can demoralize and destroy an entire country.

Corruption takes away the integrity of a country's government. Corruption breathes unrest amongst the people and in the end it will be the people of that country that will get the short end of the stick. Dictators are worse they are not concerned about people at all nor the country itself, they're only interested in wealth and power. These monsters keenly know that there word is ultimately the law. A dictator knows he have the power to execute anyone who transgress against his law. To make a point dictators will systematically have woman and children killed for no reason at all and yet still be able to sleep well at night. What a monstrosity of inhumane behavior concerning people and their right to live. People are enslaved even in 2010 in some countries and sold for money. Right now there is an epidemic of child sex trafficking. Corrupt men and women steal children as little as three years old and sell them for sexual profits all over the world. Children at this age are in high demands for demonic people that have this lustful greed to have sex with children.

This sickens me at times when I think about the children involved. At times I become so emotionally charged that I have to take deep breaths to get myself composed again when I think about this terrible thing. I remember watching a documentary on children sex trade. The documentary explained how children were being targeted for sex. This documentary captured the live scenes of the dilapidated houses that the children were being housed in. It showed how 50 to 60 children were housed in one house. It went on to show how young and old men came in and picked the child he wanted to spend time with.

It also showed the keeper of the house gesturing to the children to make sexual flirtation towards the men that came in. Some footage showed how the children became ecstatic at the fact that they were being single out to have sex with a man that might have been in his late forties. This is so demonic, so completely evil and horrifying at the same time. I ask how can men look past the possibility that one day this may very well be one of their nieces or nephews being subjected to something as evil and unnatural. The children were crammed in terrible housing arrangements, and the men went along as thou this was something totally natural. This story I witnessed really tore at my soul for a long time. I was actually hurt and ashamed because I couldn't do anything about it at the moment. How can people take tender children and use them for their pleasure in such a terrible way?

How without a second thought take away their innocence in such an inhumane way? How was it possible for these evil men who had no remorse, look in their faces and not see the hopelessness of their situation? Instead the men allowed themselves to actually in all reality rape the children. To me this is just inconceivable for a man of this age to do such a thing. Who ever purchase a copy of this book or whoever is reading this book right now at this moment, I ask please pray for the children who are literally being used in every ungodly manner. We are the voice of the children so we pray without ceasing for the children and for their deliverance from this evil society of extreme greedy people. I ask with my whole heart that you pray. Oh God Please Pray!!

There is also a spirit of reckless gambling that many has fell victim to. The reckless greed for gambling has left a lasting mark on our society. The victims of this spirit have witnessed great misfortunes in their lives. Many now experience the loss of all their worldly possession, as well as the lost of their families. Whole families have been subjected to homelessness because of this extreme desire to gamble. I just want to say that everything is so out of control we need our God right now. Man has allowed himself to be demonically influenced by the Devil of this world. In so many aspects in human life, the Devil has influenced this world with extreme evil. His assault on man desires is relentless and thorough in every degree.

He has challenged man desire since the very beginning. He has fatally twisted, and turned man's desires into the most hideous picture of evil. Satan has perfectly disguised evil as good and good as evil. He is a master at deception whether the deception is in the spirit or in our own flesh. Satan is truly a genuine master at this deceptive assault on God's people and the people of the world. His most convincing way to sell his deception is in the desire of men. Philip.4 1-6 tells us how to defeat Satan and his tricks. The bible says be anxious for nothing but in all things with prayer and supplication with thanksgiving let your request be known on to God and the peace of God shall guard your hearts and mind in Christ Jesus.

When we allow ourselves to get over anxious with desire, our desire overtakes our emotions and eventually distorts our way. We begin to walk blindly instead of walking in faith. When we are not connected with God by our faith we do not have his protection and care and so we suffer the onslaught of Satan deception. The bible says that Satan goes out seeking whom he may devour and in my life time I come to know that this is very true. He desire to see God's people disconnected from his protection. We as God's children should learn how to be patient as we wait on our desires from God. We should learn how to restrain ourselves from desiring something that will eventually take us from the presence of God. We come to know that in God's presence lives our security, peace, joy, hope, and our expected end.

So why should we want something that God don't want for us. Should we want something that we are not prepared to wait on God to release to us? I know in my personal life when I decided to carry out rash decisions there were always pieces to pick up from the aftermath of my decisions. When God isn't in your decision making its easy to find yourself hurt and vulnerable at the end of each decision. How can I act independently knowing what is waiting for me in the aftermath of my decision when I move without God?

Satan is real and relentless and wishes you to perish. He truly wants to kill God's people, but he will take you minus a leg or a hand or anything that keeps you from being completely whole. He wants to get you into moving without God because surely after moving without God our desire starts to deteriate and finally we return back to what God has delivered us from. Sometimes the mind of God's people becomes reprobate and we go beyond what God had originally delivered us from. We begin to explore aspects of sin that God truly find horrible and an abomination in every aspect of the word. This is truly our flesh and Satan working together. The further we move from God the further the depths and the shape of sin we experience. There is no ending depth of the file things that Satan can present and will present to you if you been driven this far from God. He presents horrific things, sometimes things that haven't been thought of by the average human being. I just want you to never forget how masterful this Devil is. He is not to be taken lightly at any given time.

He is not to be praised at any given time, he is not to be felt sorry for at any given time, and we are not to give ourselves over to him at any given time. His evil work on mankind is evident all through the earth, sickness, diseases, famine, etc. All through the earth the signs of Satan are evident and overbearing. Out of evil desire millions of people has died from wars and continue to die because of men visions of conquest and personal gain. Out of evil desires great men has been murdered for issues they stood up for. Satan looks for those that are being led by their desire and not by the wisdom of God.

He loves the fact that he is able to deceive God's people to move out without his guidance and care. He loves the fact that thru the years he's been able to master the deception of disguising what is bad for good and what is good for bad. He prides himself of the fact that many of God's people has perished behind the tactics he has used thru mankind life span. The children of God that fall victim to his deceptions and perishes, Satan reminds God of it and the tears of God runs down his loving face and sorrow lives in his heart. Satan brutally consumes his victims with confusion and indecision and whirlwind them into his trap. God sees the traps and he tries to warn us but at this time we are just too vulnerable and confused to hear the voice of God. At this time we are victims that have no idea of what's going on. I know sometimes we get over anxious and we want what we want and we want it now. In our spirit we sometime get tired and weary when it gets increasingly tiresome waiting on God.

Nonetheless we have to be led by the spirit; being led by the spirit will always keep our flesh under subjection. Roman 8:14 states that those that walk by the spirit are the sons of God. Mathew 6:24 states that no man can serve two masters either he will love one and hate the other. We can not love God and the Devil at the same time. Joshua said to the people of Israel choose yea whom you will serve. For as for my house we shall serve the Lord. Don't let the Devil get your mind off God and on the desire that you crave. The Devil has become a master trickster at deceiving God's people. His desire is to see God's people return to a fleshly state as they wait on God. This is always his plan; he has become a master trickster at achieving this goal. His desire is to see us act independently from God so our lives will catastrophically spiral down to nothing.

He loves it when he is successful at achieving this goal. But we don't have to fall victim to his schemes because God always makes a way of escape for us. Even when things get really hard and we can barely see our way out; God is yet there and will always be there. When all hell is breaking loose in our lives God is yet still there. Even when it feels like our enemies has surrounded us we have come to know that God is still there and will bring us out every time if we allow him. So don't fall for Satan tricks, we wait on God and wait with patience and joy while giving God all the glory.

Our desires should be centered around our vision and the call that God has set on our lives. If our desires is centered on the call on our lives then there will be nothing lacking in our lives. Some desires that God fulfill in our lives are just too fortify the fact that he's God. God with his awesomeness will tell a person at times to present the deepest desire to him and he will bring it to pass. But ordinarily your desire is shaped around the call on your life. Their essence is derived from the love of God and your compassion for people. It simply works like this. The love of God changes lives and my testimony testifies to that and so now I want it to work for others the same way that it worked in my life.

Our desires are born from a desire to show God love and power in the most effective way. We want to present his love and power in the fullness. The bible says that in Mathew Chapt: 5 Whosoever thirst and hunger after righteousness shall be filled. So whatever you hunger for and whatever you hope for, whatever you envision shall come to pass, this is the benefits of God. God will add on to you great and awesome things. He will create Godly desires in you that will be nothing less than awesome. He is not a God that will lie or a God that needs to repent for he is faithful and will not allow his word to fail. If he said you will be fulfilled then you shall be fulfilled and left with joy.

This is the end of a person that believes God who continues down the way of righteousness, unspeakable joy he shall find. We seek God continuously because we see people needs and because of their needs we seek God in prayer for their needs to be meet. We earnestly pray and travail for the coming of Gods power that will subdue the needs of his people. Our true desire of God is that God move mightily thru the earth and bring forth the greatest revival in these last days. We who are God's children truly just want to witness God's movement in the lives of his people.

Your desire to lift up God's kingdom will surely come to pass if we continue in God's way. God will supply your need and grant your petition because of your concern for the poor in spirit. The word of God says in his word that he can do exceedingly and abundantly above all that we can ask or think. So I ask is there anything to hard for God? I shall say not. Who is it that wants to do great exploits for God? Who is it that wants to see the sick healed? Who is it that wants to see the masses delivered? Continue to serve God so he can change your life in a wonderful way. Let us not desire life just for ourselves; but let us desire life for the people of this world. Desire life for your enemies; desire that your enemy will be filled with the love of God. Have a Godly desire that God will someday save them, and ask God how you can play a part in their coming to Jesus. I know it's hard sometimes to pray for your enemies, but what is love if you love only the ones that loves you.

That's not pure love; the bible says that we should be our brother keepers. The second commandment that Jesus left with us is that we should love our neighbors as our selves. In spite of our selves we need to move beyond ourselves so we may come to know the heart of God. Beyond us is the essence of God and in God everything is good. God's heart continues to beat in our spirit as he talks to us and leads us ever so gently to heights unimaginable. He gently guides us to truth which delivers us into safety all the times. We are safe in God's arms when we seek him first and not our independent desires. Mathews 6:33 But first seek the kingdom of God and all his righteousness and all these things shall be added on to you. Seek God as you would seek for silver and gold and allow diligence to rule your heart as you press on to know him.

He is a God that wants to reveal himself to you with all splendors. You will forever be overwhelmed with awe in God's presence. His splendor will overtake you with tears of joy and amazement. So let him show you how he desires to grant you your every desire simply because you have love for him. God forever finds reason to give; he continues to show mercy to his children and to the people of the earth. He loves us and wants to take our desires to uplift the kingdom. He wants to shape your desire so you can have a reward here on earth and in heaven. Your desires are important to God and watch him fulfill every one of them. Just stay faithful.

GOD HE IS FAITHFUL

Write the Vision
Chapter Three

Dreams and Visions are necessary to the man of God and to the woman of God. Why? Because dreams and visions pave the way to the manifestation of your purpose and desires in God. Desires birth spiritual and mental pictures of your vision daily as we meditate. The more we meditate the more the pictures become a part of us. Eventually it comes to the point that our spiritual and mental pictures of our vision begin to automatically present themselves without much meditation because now our vision has been lodged into our hearts. Desire is the component which locks our vision in our hearts. In so many words desire is the heart of our vision.

Desire corners the vision and enables us to write the vision. It makes the vision or dream plain to see as if we were looking at a physical picture. Your desire from God is what gives birth to your vision or dream. It is as if desire is a pregnant woman. As the woman desire to see the child in her womb she pushes with all she has to see it. Well with our dreams and vision it is our desire that pushes the manifestation of our dreams and vision to reality. The word of God says that without vision man perishes. Why does man perish without vision? Because man cannot be held in place without vision. Vision anchors a man it stabilizes him with a yearning to bring forth. Desire creates a motivation or intensifies the hope of bringing forth the vision within us. If there's no desire to bring forth vision you can't be kept. You will never be truly stable, nor will you ever be equipped to accomplish. Have you ever had an experience with a person that was considering suicide as a way out? Well if you did then you know that the great level of confusion and stress in this person life took them to a place of no return. If you studied the mindset of a person who have choose suicide as an option you will understand there exist an voidance of vision and desire. If a person is void of vision and desire there will be minimal rationale within them. There will always be a great void when desire and vision is not present in a person. Why? Because these two essential things are the forces that keep us fighting to bring forth or at the very least it gives us desire for self preservation.

Being trapped in this position leaves the individual open to controlling spirits even a suicide spirit. But God's hope for us is that we receive his gift of life. God gives us life in abundance and truly he desire that we live it in an abundant manner. His desire for you and me is that we be well and that we prosper always. He cares about how we live and how we interact with one another, he cares about how we are rewarded for the things that we accomplish in the kingdom. He is forever watching shaping and molding us for an exalted place in which he has called us to. His thought for us is an expected end which will always result into fulfillment and unspeakable joy. But the Devil wants to bring us to the point of suicide he wants the plan of God aborted in our lives. He wants us to give in to seducing spirits, spirits that is unleashed by him to bring us down. His assignment is to take over our lives by filling us with fear and doom. The more we allow our selves to be seduced by negative aggressive feelings and thoughts the more the Devil drags us to the level of no return.

Once he gets us to this deadly point he comes with everything he got so we're not able to visualize a way out for ourselves. The Devil wants us to accept without a fight the end of us. It is so diabolical the way we are trapped off into this state of no return. It is so diabolical to find ourselves in this place and can't fight our way out. This condition comes on so subtlety but it takes on a more aggressive nature as it continues to take over us.

We allow it to take over us because of the voidance of vision and desire. Without these two essential spiritual weapons in our lives we are open for an oppress spirit to take over our lives. Not only do this spirit of hopelessness affects us it also affects the people around us. Our lives affect the people around us. When we are in trouble the people we love begin to alter their lives by implementing the necessary things that can help us in ours. It's a tragic thing for people to watch you waste away, to watch you live without buoyancy, to live without fight, to live without aggressive desire to bring forth.

Family and friends sometimes get caught up emotionally when we are going thru hard times in our lives. They suffer as we suffer through our condition. So your situation not only affects you it also affects the people that loves you. As we give power to these seducing spirits they command more territory in our lives. The affects can be tremendously wide and broad depending on what type of background we come from. Having a loving background of family and friends helps the situation. But the victims that are not fortunate to have people that they can call on will probably slip into this condition with a greater progression because there is no love to help counteract this spirit. So the victims go forward in to captivity by this spirit without restraints. Its likes riding in a car without brakes; you are going to have a tragic ending. Love slows down this condition it gives the sufferer emotional attachments; it gives reflections on past and present events of their lives. In so many words it gives the sufferer something to hang on to and if by chance they do recover it gives them the strength to reestablish their lives as well as reestablishing their vision or establishing one. This is very crucial that we have a vision for our lives. Vision is an essential weapon against the Devil and his desire to destroy us. Our vision is what helps us keep our mind in trouble times. It helps us to fight for peace in trouble times. It gives comfort as we think about the things we want to do for God. It gives hope as we think about our assignment that God has entrusted us with. However when God shows us vision there should be a certain amount of joy that will enables us to walk out the things of God. I want to endure the things that I fight against in my everyday life.

I have to endure situations, situations that may occur on my job. I must be able to ride the storms in my marriage. I must trust God enough to know that he will give me the victory over anything that may come against me. I don't want to be caught in the enemy camp and taken advantage of. I don't want to allow him to deceive me into a condition where I can't see my way out. I come to know that there is many spirits that can overtake you when you are experiencing this level of hell in your life. The spirit of addiction can arise from this matter. This spirit can come in the form of sex, violence drugs and in many other assorted ways. If you were to research a person who has developed an addiction problem, you would come to conclude that the person either never had a vision established or they took their eyes off their vision and lost focus. It is so very easy to loose focus and the Devil is counting on it.

He is counting on us to take our eyes off God. His desire is that we begin living an independent life separated from God. He knows if we edge God out of our lives we will not have God's covering and his protection in our lives. A man without vision or a person that has lost focus of their vision is subject to a spirit of addiction. One of the symptoms of this condition is extremity. If a person gambled and was captured by this spirit of addiction he will gamble at all cost. He will gamble even at the expense of losing his family and every worldly possession. This person will continue to gamble because of the void in his or her life. They will gamble because they refuse to ask for help to help combat this condition.

This void can come very easy in a person life. Case scenario: If a couple married and had marital problems and if he or she gambled whenever the couple had a fight or argued there is a possibility that this person may easily begin to rely on gambling as an answer to their problems rather than dealing with his or her marriage. Neglecting and avoiding problems tends to gravitate us to what interest us the most. If the wife or husband is seen as a hindrance or a nuisance they may easily fall in the trap of gambling to the extreme, meaning gambling at all cost. It will become comfortably easy to gamble when the couple experience martial problems. Eventually this person may easily become addicted to gambling and thus be brought to destruction by making the decision to gamble. Addiction is a devastating spirit it rules the person three folds, spiritually, mentally and physically. The person is driven to levels of emotional stress and despair that is almost unthinkable.

The things people do when captured by an addictive spirit is truly sometimes unimaginable. This spirit command attention at all times. It is a restless spirit that continues to drag the victim to lower levels of shame, guilt and every other demeaning word that describes the state of the addictive person. Addiction changes the personality of a person and even changes their full character after a long period of time. Unless the person seeks help from God he is unable to arrest this spirit. At this level anything is possible, meaning that the person is truly unpredictable and truly grossly unstable. There is no stabilization in his or her life. He or she becomes open to just about anything that is self inflicting, this is truly a slow way of suicide. Having no spiritual help is detrimental and can easily lead you to death.

In this condition people find themselves in the wrong places doing the wrong things sometimes without any remorse. It is a sad thing to see someone so thoroughly used by the Devil. To actually see someone that might have been really vibrant and healthy and even very helpful to others become depleted of vital sign of life by an addictive spirit is truly saddening. It is truly an evil transformation that occurs. At times the person takes the form of the spirit physically. The contours of the face begin to outline the spirit that is within. Crack Cocaine is a restless spirit and so the person contours of his or her face reveal restlessness. I guess

I'm writing about addiction because I come to know that anyone can be overtaken if you don't stay focused, or continue working towards manifesting your vision in the physical realm. I just need to say that Satan wants to see us out of place. He wants to see us independent from God. He is always on the horizon seeking whom he may devour. He has done this time and time again. He is a master at finding ways to oppress us into giving into his ways.

He uses anything and anybody that is willing to do his bidding he does not care. I just want to reiterate that he is ruthless and thorough when it comes to deceiving and manipulating you if you allow him in. It is only when we allow him in that he has room to do such things. It's only when we allow him in does he has any authority to implements this plan that has caused many to perish and even the children of God. The children of God perish because we don't acknowledge God guidance nor do we use the power of our weapons we have been given that destroys whatever weapons that is formed against us.

When we don't carefully use what we have been taught we are overtaken as well. If we do not use our weapons to destroy the Devil plans, this is the waiting dilemma for all those that are overtaken. It may not be addiction that overtakes you, but you will find that the Devil once he has you even for a little while will abuse you thoroughly in every part of your life until you find focus again. He is truly an opportunist he waits and waits patiently for his victims and with great precision which he has obtained over centuries of practice.

Time after time he destroys people lives in a blink of an eye. Total destruction is what he seeks but like I explained in the book earlier he will be happy just to be able to destroy your life as much as he can. The love of God, desire, purpose and vision eradicate the Devil infiltration into our lives. He cannot break the barricade of love of a Saint that has fallen in love with God. He cannot break the barricade of those who are very attentive to their spiritual condition. Those that have love for God and wish to be used by God do examine their lives constantly because desire, purpose and vision are always before them. Examining themselves keeps them keenly motivated in the work of the kingdom. This in turn keeps their minds from being overtaken by this spirit. Our weapons are not carnal they are mighty in destroying strongholds and every situation that comes up against us.

Without a vision from God we perish. Vision is a weapon that grounds a Saint. One important thing about vision it is always on the offense. It is always moving forward, it is forever perking us up when we get down a little. When we get down in our spirit our vision begin to show us that nothing is more important than the things that God has entrusted us with. It refreshes us to know that we are one of God trusted servant that will make a difference in the world. We are God's chosen that will implement change in this world regardless of how minute it may be we are yet still chosen to do such a thing or things. Vision is the key to our work because vision enhances compassion and every where we go there is a need for compassion. Need is the foundation of our vision.

God gives you vision because of the enormous need in the world. He does not give us vision so we can compare vision with each other. He gives us vision to be a vessel of help to those in need. We sometimes want to compare ourselves to each other which is simply useless and prideful. We sometimes forget that it's God that gives us the power to do what we do. It's him that gives us direction and the strength to do the things that we do for him and for the kingdom. God is all that we need to live a victorious life in Christ. We do not have to compare ourselves with each other this is a trick of the Devil.

It's a trick that's been used against the children of God by the Devil since the time of Cain and Abel. Cain compared himself with Abel and the outcome was disastrous. Let us as Saints of God come to know the very revelation in God, the revelation of knowing that what God has for me is for me. He will always be ever generous towards us. Surely there is no reason for us to fight and conjure up jealousy and strife between each other. We are magnificent people and thoroughly blessed by God in ever way possible. So let us all bless God for the very things that he has given us and the things that he is going to bestow upon us. We are blessed people beyond our imagination. The word of God reveals that he can do exceedingly and abundantly above all that we can ask and think. The best thing about this statement is that we can not even think beyond God's power and strength.

So who can stand against us, who can form weapons that can prevail against the children of God?
I say emphatically no one or nothing can stand against us because God is all powerful, all wonderful and all protective of his people. I say praise with those that is with you when God bless them, praise an honest praise because truly we should want to see our brothers and sisters blessed. I come to know that whatever or however we are blessed by God it is always to lift him up and to glorify him for his awesome love and grace he bestows upon us. We lift him up and glorify him because we love him. We love him because of the mighty changes he made manifest in our lives. He commands opportunities to reveal himself to the earth in a personal way.

Vision is the spiritual vessel that he uses to make himself known in a more personal manner. He desire that we write down our vision so we'll be able to see his working in our life. Knowing that God is working in our lives proves God on a more personal level. When he begins bringing forth the vision that is written in our hearts it stretches our relationship with him. God may give you the full vision all at once, or he may give it to you by sections. But however he may give it you want to write it down so you can see him perform his great wonders in your life. The things that God does for you and in you are going to continue to bring you closer to him. He wants to be known to you on a more personal basis. He will always show you many ways that will lead you to trust him even more. God will do unexpected things in your life that will solidify his presence and his love. God proves himself in accordance to his word.

Your vision is personal to him he knows that not only will it create a bond between you and him, but it will also connect you with a network of people which God has called you to. Vision is manifested by God but God has called a network of people to bring it forth in the physical world. Yes it is your purpose, desire and vision but God has called specific people to your life to help bring it to past. There is one thing that is vital about bringing forth vision, you cannot bring vision forth alone. It is not just to bless you as I explained earlier. Your vision is going to touch not just your life but many others. Whatever God does is blessed so shall all the partakers that share in his mighty works.

So all that network and share in the vision which God has entrusted in you shall be blessed. They shall be thoroughly empowered by God because they were obedient to lend themselves to help you bring forth vision. You must remember that the people assigned to your work are vital to your vision. God has given certain people gifts to enhance your life. God has assigned people to you that will help you discern certain things in your life. There are prophets that God assigned to you that can give you a word in season. Prayer warriors that God will lay on their heart to continuously pray for you. God has also put in certain people heart to bless you financially.

God has lain on the heart of certain financial institutions to bless you with the finances you will need to fulfill your vision. God will bless you because you have showed willingness to bring forth that which he has entrusted you with. So as you determine yourself to walk out this mighty vision God blesses you in the process. He pours his heart out to you and holds you to himself and makes manifest all the things you ever wanted appear before your very eyes. So it behooves you and I to hear God and adjust to his will. Walking in God Will will always give us the comfort of knowing that we are blessed people. What greater way to live, to live and know that you are walking in a bless state. Blessed continuously!

You will always know that you are blessed as God put the pieces of your vision together. Seeing the vision coming together is enough to shout and praise God all day and night. There is an excitement as he put the necessary people in your life to help bring the vision to pass. As God brings sections of your vision together every now and then God will reveal to you people that will be part of your spiritual equation. He will reveal to you specifically the roles they will play. If he introduces you to a person that is to pray for you daily he will make it known to you by discernment. Sometimes God will not allow you to meet the person, he will only allow you to know that this person has a role in your pursuit. Of course he knows that we are human and so he will allow the physical attachments to take affect also. God knows that relationships are mighty when it comes to networking and accomplishing. He knows there is strength in numbers when there are likeminded people in the equation.

There is times when we must touch and agree on certain issues that arise. We should want to touch and agree with those that have a heart for us, people who knows what we are facing. We want to touch and agree with people that knows what we contend with on a daily basis. We must understand that relationships help us to turn from isolation and in turn keeps us from feeling like we have to make everything happen on our own. God wants you to make yourself known to certain people who he has strategically ordained to help you.

Remember God loves you and desire that not only do you receive his love but also the love from those that you interact with as human being. This is also a valuable part of the process, receiving strength from one another by interaction. If God call you to build things and if he called you to be a lender well then you must have financing. There must be a flow of money going in and out. It cost to feed the hungry, it cost to shelter the homeless, and it cost to finance crusades etc. There is a cost to our vision and God has a plan to bring it to pass. He has ordained institutions to furnish you with financing; he has willed that certain people in ministry help you with financing. Your vision will touch many people and many will donate their finances and time to help you bring forth the vision that is in you. He desires your vision to reach as many people as it possibly can. God knows that whomever it reaches they will become potentially helpers and workers. In so many words people will unite with you because of the love they have for God. They know that the work they put forth will meet many needs in the world.

Why do we write the vision down? So we can explain our vision to potential workers and helpers. It's like a business plan you reveal to a lender. You show the vision and the guidelines in what you hope to accomplish. You want to be able to show how you will profit from this plan; you also want to show how you will strategically be able to pay back the financial institution. We should always be clear about certain things. I know God sometimes don't make things really clear to us at times but eventually he reveals those things and we write them down and keep a record of what he has shown us. This is vital to God adding on to our purpose. This process will truly stretch our relationship with God. God wants to amaze us as he put all the working pieces together. You know to actually hear God tell you something or actually show you what he is going to do and then bring it to pass is astonishing. So if it is written on your heart well then you know that God has done what he said he will do. This is what you reveal to people who will become potential co workers with you, you want to let them know what God has already done and then be able to show them just that. This will be a testament that God is truly working in your life. Understanding that networking is key to your Christian life will eliminate the stress of receiving from God. If you look at God's children as men of God and women of God without prejudice, without judging, without pride well then you will be able to understand that God has people that will bless you. We have problems with this revelation because of our human traits at times.

 Our humanness will allow us to judge the outside of a person and not the inside or should I say the spirit of a person. When we don't judge people by God's leading this will cause us to conclude that the person is not capable to bless us in any way possible. But God has people that will walk right up to us and tell us that God said to bless you with this. There are people that God will lay on their hearts to get out of their cars and give it to one of God's children right on the spot. When the person receives the car they automatically know that it is from the Lord without the giver even revealing it.

God's people bless others everyday unexpectedly simply because they want to be obedient in what God has asked them to do. They want to bless you as much as God want to bless you. They give to you because they know that God is going to bless them in return. In so many words God's people want to bless your socks off. They understand that blessing you will be blessing themselves. God loves a cheerful giver and if you give cheerfully without anger, then God will bless you beyond your imagination. I think about the widow woman with the one mite. The one mite was all she had and she gave it thankfully. The Pharisees also gave but they gave out of pride and abundance. Jesus said that the woman with the mite was blessed far more than the Pharisee's who gave out of abundance and pride. This woman was blessed immensely because she gave out of a pure heart.

It's really a tragedy to give and it not be recognized by God. God is attentive to all that we do; he considers our labor we do in the kingdom. I believe that it sadden God to see his children give and not give with a cheerful demeanor. God wants to bless us for the love that we display in his name. He actually wants the opportunity to be able to bless you and to give you your heart desire. In fact he longs to bless you without measure. The word of God in the book of Malachi states that God is ready to open the windows of heaven if we conduct ourselves in giving as it is written in the word of God. People that give to us have a real understanding of how important it is to build God's kingdom.

They understand that giving to one another is key in kingdom building and so the bless people of God do not shy away when the opportunity to give comes around. In fact they wait for opportunities to give and when they give they often give beyond their capacity. They know that sacrifice is truly something that moves God. Giving beyond in spite of the situation that you may find yourself in is a sweet smelling aroma to God. If you ever want to get God's attention then give when your situation tells you that you shouldn't give. Give when you know that rent is due and all sorts of other bills are due to be paid. Give when you want to really use the money to buy

something new you been saving up for and then watch how God blesses you. What you sow is surely what you shall reap and this is my experience in life. I get back what I sow and I get it in abundance with God. God loves to give you in abundance and he explains this so very carefully in the word of God. The word of God says that however you sow this is how you shall reap. He explains that if you sow sparingly then you shall reap sparingly, and if you sow abundantly well then you shall reap abundantly. He wants you to get into the habit of being a person that sows abundantly so he can bless you in abundance. The question is always before you and me. How much do we really want to be blessed?

Your giving will show how much you really want to be blessed. So I am saying all this just to remind you that God has moved on people hearts to help finance your vision. A person that has been assigned to you knows the benefits of giving to you. They know God is going to bless them a 100 times over. They know it moves God joyfully when they give with a cheerful heart. They already understand that their giving to you will bless them and so they will seek opportunities to do just that. Remember always that God will use anybody and anything to bless you. Do not take anybody or anything for granted. But hear from God about those that he would put into your life to help bring your vision

to life. This is extremely important to pray continually concerning this very thing. Because the next person that God puts into your life may be the key to your whole vision unfolding right before your eyes. People are monumental to this matter simply because people are key. Using people is how God gets his work done on earth. God wants to use key people to link together to do marvelous things here on earth. He really enjoys watching people work together because he is a God that love relationship. So once again people is key, writing the vision down and giving with a cheerful heart are keys also to seeing your vision come to pass. Without these keys there is a good chance that your vision won't produce fully as God attended it to do. When making a cake you always want to know the ingredients that goes into making it. You want to be very careful that you have the right ingredients in order to be successful. Each ingredient is vital and necessary to producing the cake, and so with focus and intent we search out the ingredients. The same with our vision we search out the things that God intends to use to bring it to past. We allow God to lead us to those vital things that will help our vision come to life. We allow him to show us the people whom he desires us to form relationships with. We allow people to bless us and take none of God's people for granted, remembering that God will use anybody and anything to help us. But most important write the vision down so you'll be able to explain it to potential co workers.

We run with diligence and faith to see our vision accomplished. We run with patience so that our labor will never be in vain. And we pray for strength to accomplish the task before us. But most importantly we pray for all people especially the children of God.

LET'S GIVE HIM A PRAISE

Calling Forth Those Things
Chapter Four

Another critical aspect concerning our vision is speaking. We must speak forth our vision; we must speak forth our heart desire. We should always speak that which we desire to happen in our lives. If you want blessing to manifest in your life start speaking them into your life. The bible tells us to speak those things that are not as if there already are. So from that alone tells us that speaking has power whether we speak positive or negative. So it would be wise to always speak things that are good. When the Lord spoke everything in existence in the beginning he declared it all good. Everything has it beginning in God's speaking except the making of man. In making man God actually used his Godly hands to make man. He took his hands and molded man into his image and then God inserted life into man. God spoke the entire universe in existence and said it was good which should stand as an example of the power that we have. We have inherited this same power from God because God working power abides in us.

We do have the power of life and death in our tongues or should I say our mouth. We can speak life into our situation or we can speak death into our situation. We are given a choice to speak blessings or curses. What should we speak? We should speak those things that we envision, the same vision that God has given to us. Purpose, desire, and vision are the ingredients that bring forth life as we speak. Purpose bring desire, desire bring vision and now vision demands for it to be called out. This is why it is so important that you write down the vision in your heart or physically write it down. Having the vision written down or securely having it lodged in our heart will enable us to call if forth. We want to study our vision; our vision should become a part of us. I come to know that the way something becomes a part of us is that we must spend time with it. We must spend time meditating and speaking about our vision. We need to study our vision until we see mental pictures of it on a daily basis. We need to see this set of pictures in our prayers, on our jobs, wherever we may find ourselves, somehow our vision must become a part of us. When the vision becomes a part of us, speaking about it becomes an automatic exercise to us. We understand at this time how vital it is to meditate on our vision and how equally important it is to speak it forth. The more we meditate and speak about our vision we will come to find out that the mental pictures we now have of our vision will automatically begin to enter our minds without using much meditation to bring them about. When something is always before you it is hard to overlook it. When something is always in your face it is much easier to acknowledge it.

Meditating on your vision daily creates unction in your spirit to speak it forth. Meditation creates unction or a silent desperate desire to see it come to pass into the physical world. A vision is good when it's spiritually inside of you but it serves a greater purpose when we are able to bring it to pass. And the only scriptural way that I know that will bring it to the physical world is to keep speaking about the vision.

We can begin speaking about it with our families and friends; we can even speak to God about it in our prayers. We can speak to ourselves about our vision which will encourage us in our hard times. Sometimes when we are going thru difficult situations we can go over the plan that God has for our lives this will help restore our joy. As our joy is being restored waves of excitement fills our drained bodies and cloudy minds. We can feel life rushing into our spiritual blood stream and into our physical body. We find ourselves ready to enter into the fight once again. Knowing the restoring power of our vision gives us a greater understanding of the Holy Ghost power that lives within us. God is confident about the vision he has given you and the words of encouragement he has spoken in your life. His word is all that we need to make it thru; his word is more than able to bring us out. The word of God comforts us as we speak forth; it has a comforting power which helps us not to be overwhelmed by the magnitude of our vision in which we speak about.

I know difficult times and situations create fear and we may find ourselves paralyzed by this gripping spirit {fear}. Fear will eat at our faith if we allow it to. But we learn to rebuke the Devil until our faith return to us. This lesson takes time to learn, the lesson of resisting the Devil. If you continue to call on God in your hard times the Devil can do nothing but leave the presence of God. He cannot stand truth because he is a liar. He cannot stand in the presence of holiness because he is evil.

Learn the lesson of calling on God in your troubles and watch the Devil flee every time. In our hard times it's difficult to speak such lofty things, we find it hard to believe such things ourselves when we are faced with such tremendous trails.

But I say continue to speak anyway, speak until the cows come home. Speak until you no longer have a voice, I don't care what happen do not let the Devil close your mouth. Continue to reveal the vision that God has entrusted you with. Remember the Devil plan is to stop you from speaking forth that precious thing inside of you (vision). He is fully determined to steal the plan of God for your life. This is why we must listen for God's voice; we must listen for God's voice especially in our trouble times. In trouble times it will be God's voice and the remembrance of your vision that will help restore your faith. It is difficult to speak about a great future when you have outstanding bills that need to be paid such as your mortgage, or maybe the bank may be threatening to take away your house. You may have worked at a job for a long period of time and the company has called you in the office and explained to you that the company is shutting down for various reasons.

Maybe you found out that your spouse cheated on you and is still cheating. Situations like this are hard to endure; you will need all the help and encouragement from God to make it thru. It can really become difficult at times confessing what we can't see as opposed to what we can see. In times like this it's very easy to start confessing the negative things that we see. Times like this we can easily begin to ask ourselves if we really believe the very thing that we speak about so passionately. .

Sometimes it feels like the enemy has us totally surrounded in trouble. We find out that the more we confess and speak about the vision that God has given to us the more trouble and stress increases. But God understand the problem and in due time he sends his word to bring us relief in our situations if we allow it to. It can really be very hard emotionally and spiritually in these incredible hard times, the only way to survive is to hear from God. The Lord is going to always let us know that he's there with us all the way. Satan wants to tie your tongue from speaking, he will try to infiltrate your mind and pollute it with thoughts that does not glorify or edify God. In fact he wants you to start blaming God for every wrong thing you see going on in your life. He wants you to start speaking against God in your quiet times, he wants you to ponder over the situations and then set blame to the way God is taking you. The Devil desires you to start accusing God of being a hard task master. He doesn't want us to understand that God is maturing us in our hard times.

He wants us to think we are cursed when great opposition comes against what we say we believe. I don't know how many times I have heard from people who God had in the waiting state explain to me that they believe they're cursed. This is truly a trick of the Devil, the Devil is shrewd and unyielding, he is a foe that never gives up. He knows how to wait us out, he knows precisely when to attack us. Believe me the Devil knows us well. I heard a Preacher say that the Devil knows just what you like. The Devils knows what God have delivered you from. But he will undoubtedly try to tempt you in the same area God has brought you out of. In other words Satan desire is to break you down he wants you confused about the delivering power of God. He desires you to return back from where God has brought you from.

He will do anything to undermine your confession concerning your vision. He will do any and everything to stop you from expressing the things God has encouraged you to speak into the atmosphere. He is ruthless and relentless in trying to steal the precious things that God has lodged in your heart. He knows that speaking gives life to the dreams and visions that God has ordained to come forth from you. He will not stand on the side in peace and watch you commit your vision into the physical world. He is forever seeking whom he may devour. He will kill and destroy if he is giving the chance. This is why when he has us in the vice of sin he urges us into deeper depths. He urges us deeper because he doesn't want us to understand the calling on our life nor the strength of our confession. He knows sin will surely keep our mouth closed. He wants us ignorant to the fact that everything has process in the kingdom of God. This process sometimes takes time and it takes enduring God's molding in our lives. It's hard to endure at times, let's face it we are human who has emotions we are not robots. Because we are human situations can hurt us dearly and completely. Our emotions play a big deal in whether we are going to express the things of God. Emotions that are out of control are subject to any and everything. The

Devil runs rampant through our emotions. He waits to see how emotional we get as we go thru our hard periods in life. He knows if he can attack and extort our emotions, we won't endure to the point of manifestation. He wants to keep the revelation from us that God is using the difficult things that is present in our lives to make us stronger. When God is taking us thru our situations, he doesn't take us thru to hurt us, his desire is always to make us unmovable. But God cannot get us to this place if we allow Satan to steal our confession. We must continue to keep speaking in faith if we are ever going to come to the place of manifestation. Without faith we will never see what we desire in our heart.

Faith is the substance of things hoped for the evidence of things unseen. Whatever we hoped for we must confess it, whatever we see in the spirit is the evidence of it existence. Don't blame God when he starts stretching your faith at certain times. Our faith need to be stretched it will help us learn how to endure in our trying times. In our trying times are the times we are made strong. In our trying times our endurance is stretched to the limit. But the more we can endure the less of a chance the Devil will have to change our minds about God. If we change our mind about God and his power it will eventually leads us back into sin. Faith will keep our mouth open; faith will keep us confessing without ceasing. Faith will make us yell to the world about what God is doing and what God is going to do in our lives.

It will make us shout it out from the roof top, on the train, on the bus, on our jobs etc. So we must endure and continue to endure because so much is riding on just that. We must endure until we see our vision come to pass. We cannot let the Devil have his way with us he will steal our vision. He will kill us if we allow him to prosper in our lives. A little here and a little there and eventually he has taken control of us. But the object is to never let him in even a little. Everything starts off with a little, a little doubt here and he is in, a little doubt there and he is controlling us and eventually he steals our confession and at that moment our faith stops working. Instead of serving God with joy he wants us to become irritable and emotional. But I come to know that if your joy has been stolen you will return to the things that you were familiar with in the past.

You will begin to cling to the things that brought you comfort. Refusing to go on with God is truly a grave mistake. Without God the Devil automatically returns and when he returns he returns with a vengeance. He will ban barge you with every trick and deception to keep you from returning to the safety of our Lord. I just need to let you know that you can not be neutral in God. You can not stand in the middle there is no such thing as being in the middle with God. You must understand that as a child of God if we are not advancing in the Lord well then we are retreating. It may not feel like we are retreating at first. But given a little time we will see we have stopped doing some of the things we have become accustomed to doing when we came to God. We will begin to see how our faith has eroded in areas of our life.

If we started our day seeking God in the morning we will see how our time with him has eroded. God will show us how we allowed excuses to stop our pursuit of him. If we read our bible twice a day or maybe carried our bible with us, we will see that a day at a time we have discontinued doing these vital things. Our prayers will dwindle, we will stop spending time with God and eventually our faith fails us. With the help of God we will come to know we allowed ourselves to enter into an emotional state rather than continuing to hold our spiritual ground. Our emotions are always a breathing ground for deceptions and manipulation by the Devil. We need to continue to do the things of God that kept us or keeps us growing and advancing in the great things that we come to know about him.

If we sought God in the morning then let us continue to seek him in the morning, and if we carried our bibles wherever we went then let us continue to live in that same mind frame. We want to be undeniable free to confess those things in which we know shall manifest. I don't want to be caught saying maybe he will do a thing or lacking endurance in waiting for manifestation. Let us not be deceived by the wicked one, he is the author of confusion. His nature and his call is truly to confuse and distort the picture that we have of God. He genuinely wants to make us see God as a God that will not grant what he said he will. He wants us to see God as someone that does not keep his promises. He wants us to fall out of love with the word and with God. He knows if we fall out of love with him we will stop desiring relationship with him.

To not have relationship with God means we have relationship with the world and to have relationship with the world is having relationship with death. Life and death cannot exist in the same space. The Word of God says that how can a spring have sweet and bitter water at the same time. How can we bless each other at one moment and then turn around and curse each other the next. We need to strengthen our relationship with God on a daily basis. This should be our plan for defeating the enemy, a healthy honest relationship with the Lord. We want to get used to calling on God at any giving time. Sometimes people just want to pray in their prayer closet, that's alright but when the enemy is stalking it isn't any time to think about your prayer closet you need to call on God right then and there. God is able to hear from you from your prayer closet or wherever you may be. Remember God is everywhere and sees everything and is able to deliver you from anything in a twinkling of an eye that's just how great God is.

So whatever problem you may have remember he is an anytime God, we don't have to wait for a special time to call on God. His spiritual phone is always free; you don't ever have to worry about a busy signal, nor someone hanging up. How do I know? I called him and I was able to get him when I was going thru my situations. I called him and he showed up. And when he shows up we know that he takes care of business, whatever the problem he takes care of it. I come to realize that freedom is the atmosphere for manifestation. Freedom is the remedy which will allow us to continue confession of our vision.

I remember being locked up in jail, and in jail I thought about some of the things I wanted to do when I finished the sentence I was given. I confessed that some areas in my life were going to change upon my release. So as a follow up I continued to reveal my desires to my friends and acquaintances in the community. Before I knew it I was accomplishing the things I confessed. The more I confessed the more I was motivated to bring my desires to life. The more I confessed my desires the more I accomplished. Remember always there's power in our words, our words will shape our future or utterly destroy it. If we confess what we envision the universe has to line up according to what we speak. In Genesis everything lined up for God and so will everything line up for you. We have the power in us to shape and mold whatever future we desire, we have the power to control our outcome. If we confess and continue to stand on the promises of God nothing can or nothing will be able to detour the things in which we so confess into the atmosphere. This is one of God's greatest principles the power to speak and to bring forth.

What is significant about this is that this principle works whether you are saved or not. This dynamic principle works for the saved and the unsaved. The world has borrowed this principle from God and gotten very learned in it. Because the people of the world have exercised this principle they bring forth manifestation. The bible says that God rains on the just as well as the unjust. It says that he maketh the sun to shine on the good as well as the evil. This tells me that this principle work for all those who are willing to take a hold to them. If the world knew just how much God plays a role in every aspect of life they might be more subjected and more in awe of God. But because they don't see the magnificence and the awesome wonder of a God that is generous and merciful and patient they will never know how the principles of God truly work. They might know the principals of God works but to know who makes them work is a whole different ballgame.

To know that God is the power behind any force is the pinnacle of knowledge. There is no greater knowledge than to know that God is the power behind the awesomeness of all things, whether created or spiritual. He is the creator and is surely the God that put all principles in place. We that are saved live by these principals and have full fellowship with God. But the world only have knowledge of these principals it lacks the experience and the fellowship of an almighty powerful God. Because the world will not commit to know him he has set boundaries or should I say standards that will keep the world from knowing him unless they submit to him. But we that are saved have the privilege to move past the boundaries and into God's chamber where God reveals his secrets things. So knowing what I do for God and the results that it will bring are pretty wonderful. People of the world believe if they live a clean life according to their standards will someday inherit something great when they die. But God has revealed to his people that if we lived a clean and holy life in God and not according to our standard of cleanliness we will inherit the kingdom of God. This is one of God secrets that the world doesn't know. They may hear about these things but know them they do not. This is the difference between the confession of God's people and the confession of the world. What we confess are eternal things which has great rewards attached to them. Again I want to say what if a man gains the whole world and loses his soul? The world has no right to eternity, the bible says that everything shall perish and pass away before God's word fails. So anything that exists outside the kingdom of God shall fail and will soon cease to exist.

I'm definitely happy to know that the things that I participated in spiritually have given me eternal life and not only eternal life but also rewards when I get to the place which I am called to which is heaven. But let us come to know God here on earth and come to know him and the power of our confession which is highly spiritual. But let us know that our confession will manifest itself out in the physical realm. The magician says I can make a rabbit disappear right before your eyes and he does it. And this is the way God is, you call it and he will make it appear right before your eyes. It may not be just that fast or instantaneously but it will show up, because God is good like that. I want you to understand something about God,

God want us blessed in every aspect of our lives he will do whatever it takes to get us to that place where we are fully blessed. You will know you are blessed when you learn to wait on God and his timing. God doesn't care how much you confess or call but he is only interested in when you do call or confess can you wait on the manifestation. This is the process and no one can pass by this process that God has set up for his children. We have to learn to wait on God. Sure there is fire in the blessing, but not even the fire can stop the children of God. This is a testament to the children of God, we know if we wait on God he will bring our petition to pass. The very strong things sometime will stop us from confessing and calling forth. Sure that is part of the dilemma of faith, believing when it just seem so impossible. But it wows God to see his children confessing and desiring such great things and it moves him to joy to know that he or she will surely wait for the desired petitions to come to pass.

God already knows who's going to wait patiently and not give ground to the Devil; he knows who his children are that have their mind made up to wait for his timing and process. He knows the amount of stress and pain that is ordained to our confession. He knows what we have to endure before our request is given over to us. But surely God is saying confess anyway, cry out any way, speak forth anyway, because I will accomplish this very thing. You know the greatest revelation I have received since being saved is the fact that trouble don't last always.

I have come to know that if I humble myself God will relieve all my stress and worry if I just keep it in his hand. He will surely make me free but we will never know this if we don't give ourselves to God in the time of our trouble and need. We suffer when we don't understand that God will supply our every need. We truly suffer when we don't understand that God will never let us down. We suffer when we don't have the power to wait on God's manifestation in our lives. We truly suffer when we don't understand that God will not let us go without. He will not let us go without the things we need to operate in this body. If we burn in our body, he will supply a mate for us. If we need sufficient housing he will supply it for us. If we need joy or whatever the need might be God will supply our needs. When we truly realize God will supply our needs this frees us from worldly dominated goals.

God wants us free to operate tirelessly and unburdened by needs. He wants you to be at your highest spiritual peak when serving him. He understands that your spiritual best is going to give you your victory every time. He knows your victory is in you knowing that he will supply your needs according to his riches and glory. God will take care of you, don't get it twisted. He has taken care of you so far, what make you think he's going to stop. Taking care of yourself and the stress of taking care of yourself leaves no room for investigating the pronounced and established things of God. The principals of God are greater than any worldly theory or unconcluded sayings. People find worldly theories paved in concrete, they rather go with conclusions thought up by others rather than seeking out the greater meaning of a thing. The world at times becomes belligerent when opposition comes up against their ideas. Conclusions and theories like: If you take the first step God will take two. Or the theory that states: I got to do whatever it takes to make it. People get violent and not only violent but people have been put to death because some choose to think outside the realm of accepted theory. Some burnt with fire, some shot, and some thrown to wild beast to be torn to pieces. The world wants you to accept their opinion or theory on certain matters and if you don't potentially it could easily mean your life. But many yet still are led by the spirit and they go beyond the theory of the world conclusions and they rather seek and search out answers for themselves.

Because people want to control the masses they rule with an iron hand. Many demonstrators were killed in the civil right movement because they believed that people shouldn't be segregated because of skin color. Everyone knew this law was wrong except the White Caucasians in the South. The whites in the south fought to the bitter end for something they thought was right. They didn't seem to know or just didn't care to know that segregation was wrong. Whites killed to protect this law they killed and brought violence to the movement that tried to demonstrate against it.

Violence seems to always be the answer here on earth, when someone disagrees with some conclusion that has been passed down thru the years. God don't want us to be lulled to sleep by the world, this is why he said in Proverbs, get wisdom and apply understanding. You know taking care of yourself is the trick of the enemy. He knows that if you are taking care of yourself you are not depending on God therefore that makes you self dependent. Sure that sound great and quite important and special, but being independent from God is the greatest tragedy of man. Man thrives on being independent, not answering to anyone living life as he pretty well please. The Devil wants you so busy that you can't even give God a thought. So he tricks us to seek after things independently, things that God will supply automatically. Again I say that freedom is what we seek for so we can give our all to acknowledging the will of God in our lives.

The world needs to be free from taking care of themselves and maybe some need to loose everything so they can see that God is real. The bible says let every man be a liar and let God be true. God reveal all things to us when we surrender ourselves to him. So we are free when God takes care of us and being free we are able to confess the great things that God has placed in our heart. We are free to call those things that are not as if they're already are. We come to know that we can call with confidence because God protects us and he vows that nothing will overtake us nor destroy us. So call those things forward, those things that make your heart skip a beat when you think about them in the spirit. Confess your vision whether it's big or small. Just know that God is with you and in due time he will bring it to pass. Because we are his children he will certainly bring everything to past. God is a good God; no one can beat his giving or his love for us.

Don't You Just Love Him!

Expectation:

Expectations is a word that helps us in our waiting period as we wait on God. As I explain in the recent pages of the book sometimes situations can become really emotional, and the pain of our situation can diminish our expectation concerning the things that God desires to birth into our lives. Situation can easily become really increasingly hard to hold up under and so we may find ourselves struggling to hold on to our faith. We know God will do everything that he said he would do, and he has no problem doing it and we understand this because he has done it so many times at this point in our lives. But there comes a point sometimes that even the most faithful get weary in their waiting on God. Weariness can reduce the level of your expectations. Sure God said that this thing shall come to pass, but sometimes we find ourselves asking but what about the pain right now.

Out of our emotional pain we begin to question God about the issues that's presented in our lives, even the greatest wondered sometimes. The bible talks about how Abraham and Sarah really didn't believe God about the son that the Angel of God promised them in the next year coming. In fact the bible says that Sarah laughed right in the presence of God. She didn't believe God because she let conditions rule her thinking.

She didn't allow herself to remember the impossible situations that God had already brought them through. Sarah was deceived by her present situation which was her age. She also acknowledged her husband age and came to the conclusion that both were far beyond child bearing years. Abraham himself the father of faith personally asked the Angel of God how can men at this age of 100 years old father a child. There were doubts about what God would do even when God had shown himself faithful so many times before this.

But yet concerning this one promise of God their expectation diminished because of the extenuating circumstances that prevailed in their lives. Both acknowledge their age and the period of time they waited on God to fulfill this great thing in their lives. Abraham was a man of faith this is the very reason why God choose him to receive the Promise Covenant. God told Abraham that he would bless him beyond measures if he left his kindred's and walked with him. Abraham walked with God and God blessed him and made Abraham the father of all nations. Even thou the Lord made Abraham great and brought him into the land of promise, he still couldn't believe the promise of him and Sarah his wife conceiving a baby at their advanced age.

Abraham loved God with all of his heart but yet still he was deceived by situations and conditions. God is merciful and relentless to give us our desires of our heart. So when things begin to get us down, and when our expectations gets really low at times God who is our father will have mercy upon us. God will allow something to happen in our lives that will revive our faith and our expectations in what he will do in our lives. God will allow events that will spark our fire once again. The fire is what we surely need when we encounter these low moments of expectation in our lives. We need the fire of God love and guidance that awakens us from our sleep of weariness and increasing doubt. He wants us to have our desires so bad, even when he sees us falling short in reaching for the mark. God will and always will somehow reveal ways to increase expectations in us.

Sometimes we forget it but God is faithful and just to provide us a way out, he is a father that is always attentive to our situations. He is aware of our cries, he is aware of our laughter, he is aware of our sorrow and pain, but he knows when to come to relieve us of our symptoms. Abraham was faithful but yet still failing in his faith concerning the child that God promised him and his wife Sarah. Abraham was the covenant bearer but yet he was still deceived. Abraham had everything but yet he still doubted.

When Abraham defeated the four kings who took his nephew Lot, Abraham brought back the spoils from the battle and laid them at the feet of the king of Salem. The king told Abraham to take whatever spoils he wanted to take for him and his men. Abraham told the king he wouldn't take any of the spoils; Abraham didn't want anyone to think he became rich on his own.

He wanted people to know that it was God that deserves the honor and the glory for making him rich. He gave God the glory in everything he done. But again even he yet faltered when it came to a really hard thing to believe.

Conditions and emotions will allow our expectations to decrease. We can easily be deceived at times when we pay heed to our circumstances and emotions. It will always be a tragic ending when we give in to either one of these enemies of expectation.

But the strongest enemy is our emotions, our emotions has a great bearing on the health of our expectations. Emotions lives in the flesh and faith in the spirit. If expectations has left the spirit it can no longer exist in the heart. My heart will fail if my spirit fails. My mind will fail if my spirit fails. My physical being will fail if my spirit fails. All will fail if my spirit is not holding things together. We are spiritual first and everything else follows after the leading of the spirit. The mind follows the spirit and the heart follows the spirit. So by any means if our spirit has not anchored down our emotions our mind can be deceived and our expectations can easily become diminished by the bombardment of our negative emotions.

Emotions are truly the culprit to our demise. It is the enemy that takes us out of control and ultimately takes us down. Satan desires is to drive us into an emotional state, he wants us to become antsy and impatient with the process of reaping and receiving. He knows if we are driven emotionally we can never defeat him. Emotionally we can never ward off the wiles of the Devil. His spiritual dark blows will hit its target and it will blindside us when we give in.

We will eventually be taken down because emotions have no defense against spiritual warfare. I will assure you this will always be the outcome when we fight a spiritual battle using our emotions. Emotions will make our flesh cry out; it will allow our flesh to dictate our movements in the midst of pain. Emotions must be controlled and not be allowed to dictate us in such great matters as expectation. Prosperity in our lives will only grow due to our expectation. We can have the greatest desires, we can be purposed by God, we can have the vision written down and safely secured in our heart but without the soil of expectation there will never be a harvest. We wait in vain for the desires and the requests that we have set before God. Not only do we wait in vain we suffer at levels that we shouldn't have to. Emotions is raw and without the spirit softening the blows we are hit head on and we're find ourselves tormented by every wave of emotions. The spirit reasons out the things of God, it gives us sound counsel as we trudge our way thru victorious battles.

It gives a resounding cry of praise as the flesh and the enemy attacks our knowledge of God and his most awesome power. Our spirit allows us to expect God at any given moment, at any given time. It will continue to nudge us to let us know we have a God that will never miss the mark. God can't miss the mark because he is a perfect God. He is perfect in everything that he does and will continue to be errorless now and forever more.

Wherever God has placed me only his hand and the good soil of expectation is going to bring me out or release me into that which I desire. Emotions will not bring us out; it does not have the power or the wisdom to do so. Emotions do not have the ordained power to set free.
In fact emotions will keep us in bondage without the expectation of ever getting out. Emotions is the weeds that the Devil uses as soil to plant the tares amongst the good wheat. And as you know it is hard to separate the wheat from the tares because even tares sometimes resemble wheat. If you don't take a close look at the two you can easily be deceived, you can easily be manipulated by their appearance. The only way we can be sure that our emotion isn't the spirit of God leading we must enter into the spirit and let the spirit of truth reveal the will of God. Emotions disguise itself like the spirit and hide under half truths and pride.

If we are not careful we'll be deceived by this trick of the Devil. If we do fall for this trick it's possible that the full damage of our runaway emotions will not be accessible until our emotions have fully run its course. Emotions without restraints are surely damaging. How you control your emotions will be the difference in you being great or just an average human being. Whoever can control their emotions and operate from the spirit will be great in the kingdom of God. He who is wise will be able to take the city with wisdom and patience.

How shall one take the city? They shall take the city by truth. The bible says however when the spirit of truth comes it shall guide you into all truth and it shall show you things to come. Truth will always shed light on deceptions, emotions will disguise it. Truth will always guide the man of God or the woman of God s in the way of the Lord. We want to be guided by God's leading, because the way of God is truth and his truth shall ultimately give us total victory in this life. God is the source that separates the truth from a lie. This is why we need the Holy Spirit to be the lamp unto our feet and a light unto our path. Human wisdom is surely not enough to defeat Satan and his angels of darkness. We must keep seeking God for truth, truth will clear away the deceptions of Satan it will keep our minds clear. Truth will nourish our expectations in God; it will continue to give us full confidence in knowing that God will grant our request. Emotions can destroy anyone expectation to the very point of never receiving. Abraham expectation diminished in time because his emotions overtook his faith.

His emotions attacked the expectancy of his request for a child. After a period of time his expectancy eroded because he stopped believing God. Expectancy is like jelly to peanut butter in contrast to your request from God. Expectancy is the rich soil in which your confession shall be birth from. Your confession or petition will have its time of incubation in the soil of expectancy. Your petition from God shall be nourished by expectancy as if it was the mother to your request. As the mother breastfeed her baby and nourish it with love and care, so does expectancy it nourishes your petition from God to manifestation. Expectancy comforts you when you cry at night as you wait on God. Expectancy talks to you as you encourage yourself in your waiting period. It focuses you when you get off track a little. Expectancy causes God to show up in your doubtful moments. Expectancy will cause God to show up in your weary moments. Expectancy will cause God to show up when you just feel like giving up.

Expectancy wakes you up in the morning with a happy face; it wakes you up with great hope. It gives you confidence of knowing that whatever you'll going thru at the end you will win. Yes you will win at the end because God has ordained you to win. God is not a liar nor can he lie, what God has promised will be given. He will not promise one thing and do another thing. He isn't a shifty type God; we do not have to fear God will surely give us what he promised. God is not dastardly he is neither a scenic nor does he have Alzheimer, God remember what he promised us. The Devil wants us to think that God has forgotten his promise. He wants us to think about a request that God hasn't fulfilled yet so we can start accusing God for failing on his word. But God is faithful and shall be faithful always. If we look back on our lives we will see that God has always been faithful to us and will continue to be faithful. Satan wants us to focus on our now and not our later. If given the chance he will slow down your manifestation. Don't let him disrupt you in your waiting period, in your waiting period is where you receive power and favor from God. Let us remember the people that will be affected by the release of your request from God, remember God blesses you so you can bless others. God does not bless you just for your benefit he blesses you because he has others in mind that will be blessed by him blessing you. This is not a me Gospel but a Gospel that always puts me in the back. Jesus said it's better to give than receive.

If it's better to give than receive, well then we ought to let the Holy Spirit train us to humble ourselves in greater proportions. It is going to take everything we have in Christ to win people into the kingdom considering the time we are living in. How can we begin to humble ourselves? We can humble ourselves in a greater way by sowing our time in prayer with God. Pray and continue to pray like never before knowing that your prayers are going to change things here in the earth. Volunteer at places where the needy are known to go and serve them as Jesus served his disciples as he washed their feet. Jesus washed his disciples feet to teach them that there is no big I, s or little you's. This lesson was valuable because it taught the disciples to think of the people in need and not so much of themselves. Why was this lesson so valuable? You can't concentrate on yourself when you are concentrating on others.

We concentrate on the needs of others so we don't rise up in our own pride. Assisting others will always be the remedy as a believer in Christ. Attending to others will help us not act in our own strength. We never want to act in our own strength and forget the plan of God, nor do we want to ever forget that it was God who gave us the purpose, the vision and desire for our life. God will continue to add on to us as we continue to obey him. We must become people of low degree to learn this lesson. We must cry out to God for humbleness and compassion. This will impact you and make you effective beyond measure which is something God is creating in you right now. Sitting at God feet or standing in his throne room will always humble you as you experience God. The awesomeness wills you to become greater, to become more humble, to have greater compassion and moreover to desire to be like God. Humbleness will continue to nurse our level of expectancy which is critical to our growth in God. I must expect things to turn out the way God has planned them to turn out in my life. I must trust God to help encourage me when I get weary in the waiting period of manifestation. I must yet still give God praise as the fiery trails enter into my life. I must know that God will and will always bring me out.

I must know I can trust God to do this as I hold on to my expectations while going thru my hard situations. Even thou I go through the fire I'm still free to know that soon or later God will bring me out and present me with my desired request. God is good like that!

God has entrusted us with great things, he wants us to grab a hold of them and see them to manifestation. He wants us to test him and his goodness. But we don't have to worry about it when we test God because we know that God can and will pass any test that is given to him. He isn't a God that is going to get tripped up by problems and stumbling blocks. He isn't a God that can be stopped by his enemies. He isn't a God that will falter and wimp out in the place of overwhelming conditions. But rather God is most happy when we test his love and his character; he wants us to know that his love is beyond the puny love of the world. He want us to be fully persuaded that his love is greater and most of all genuine in every aspect. We have to prove God love is greater and deeper by our action. Our action is going to show us the depths of his love and his caring. We have to live deeper in God, get closer to God, give our self more to God and thru this God is going to reveal himself in a deeper way to us. The more love we realize God is bestowing on us the more we humble ourselves so we can find ourselves patient in our waiting on him. We wait in mind knowing we will become that city built on the hill which no one can ever miss. Let our light so shine before men so they may see our good work so our father in heaven can be glorified.

The greater the humbleness the greater the father will be glorified in heaven. We just want to glorify him with everything within us. It is because of his gift of life that we have any chance to eternal life. It is because of God's love that we find ourselves safe from a horrible ending. So with that in mind don't you want to see this God who saved you with your own eyes? The bible says that we shall see him as he really is. I'm sure it's going to be a fascinating thing to see God in all of his glory.

So we continue to ask God to see more of him and he allows us to. We are blessed with the patience and endurance to wait on God with great expectations. I believe expectation is the greatest thing a Saint needs to have in this process of manifestation. Expectations will frustrate the enemy and his attempts on our life because expectation acts like a spiritual elastic shield in a Saint's life. When the enemy mounts an attack against us with his fiery darts our shield of expectation causes the darts to bounce away without full impact. When the Devil see that we can withstand his spiritual onslaught he mounts against us it frustrates him and not only do it frustrates, it also put fear in the enemy. It put the Devil in fear when he finds a Saint that understands what expectation does for them. It makes him fear when he knows that he has meet a Saint with a made up mind, a Saint that understand that God will do and will always do whatever to bring a smile and laughter to his children faces. God tells us to expect and he will do the rest. This crucial weapon allows us to wait on God even in our hard times.

We are protected; we are safe, we are confident that God has everything under control. He has the Devil under control, yes he does and the Devil knows that he does. But the problem sometimes is that we forget who God is and how marvelous his works is especially in our individual lives. We forget sometimes how marvelous our God has been in our lives and how determined he's been to change us from what we were to what we are now. Can he be anymore gracious any more merciful than he has already been? I should think not that's if you believe in eternal destiny.

What a God! How great is our God? We should thank him always and forever more. We should thank him for the calming winds he sends that changes the emotional landscape of our lives. We should thank him for the winds that come thru and brushes away the unproductive things in our lives. Sometimes to keep us going forward he sends the wind to brush away the weight that holds us down at times. Without this weight God knows it will allow us a greater experience in him. This is how we want to experience God we want to experience him in a sure way. Expectations take us to manifestation as it takes the farmer to harvest. The farmer is surely someone that knows about expectation; expectation is something that he truly lives by. The farmer knows the waiting process of manifestation. The farmer plants seed and understand there's a certain amount of time it will take before the seed bring forth its harvest.

The farmer is accustomed to waiting for the seasonal harvest; this process of waiting for harvest has taught the farmer how to conduct himself as he waits for this manifestation. When the farmer plants the seed he doesn't plant the seed with doubt nor does he plant the seed with fear, he simply plant the seed and wait on the natural process to occur. But before the farmer plant the seed there's work that he must do to the ground so that the seed can take to the ground and germinate. The farmer first has to till the ground and extract the weed so the weed will not kill the plants. After the ground has been tilled the farmer has to make sure that the seed is planted deep enough in the soil. If the seed isn't planted deep enough in the soil it will not grow properly.

For reasons like the sun will scorch the seed if the seed isn't planted deep enough or the fowls of the air will eat the seeds. There is an array of other things that a farmer does before he plants the seed. The point that I am trying to make is that the farmer has preparations before he plant the seeds. Preparations are just as important as the harvest of the plant, because the quality of the preparation will determine how healthy the harvest will be. Let' consider the soil of the ground. If the soil of the ground is parched it will be impossible to manifest a harvest because the condition of the ground isn't conducive to the seed growth.

Parched ground has no nutrients for the growth of the seed in fact parched ground holds no life. It is impossible to receive a harvest from dead soil. Dryness is considered a sign of not having life. We consider the desert as being dry and without life. It's truly to hot and too dry to grow normal plants from the soil of the desert. The ground is considered to be implantable ground because of the climate and the condition of the ground. Conditions are always key to everything that you do in life. We should always examine the condition of the things that are most important to us. We examine the condition of our house so we can get the maximized use out of it. We check for pests that may harm the foundation of the house. We check to see if there is any corrosion on the pipes and on other surface materials. We paint the house when the house begins to loose it gloss or attraction.

Some people just desire their house to look good so they can show it off. You know this is something entirely up to them as of why they consider the conditions of their house. The point is that we inspect it because the house is very important to us. Because we respect it we examine it on a daily bases, this is something that comes natural to us. Take our bank account, our bank account is something very important to us and because it is important to us we keep a very close eye on it. We keep a close eye on the amount of money we put in the account, we examine the amount of money we withdraw from the account.

We want to know the amount of money we have saved in our checking and saving accounts in case there is a need for it at any given time. We know bills are always due and must be paid in a timely fashion. We also understand crisis can come up unexpectedly and we want to be prepared for these unfortunate times in our lives. We deposit money in the account so we are able to withdraw from the account as the need arises. We inspect our account against times like this so we'll be empowered to do what we need to do financially. You know one of the worst things in life is to not to be able to move because we didn't check the condition of some aspect in our life. Checking conditions intensifies the quality of your life, because under daily examination not to many things can come up unexpectedly. Examination intensifies the level of your spiritual and emotional security.

Examination allows you to know and in turn it offers you less stress and more peace to walk thru life. When you know a thing it makes everything better. It might not seem like it's the best thing to know because of the emotional trauma it may bring. Sure knowing a thing can bring a great shock to you, but when it's all said in done in time most will say at least I know. We inspect the most important things in our life. We inspect our children because our children are important to us. So we monitor their spiritual, emotional, physical and mental state on a daily bases. We don't want anything to happen to our children so we do anything to protect them. We will always have concern about their growth in these very important areas in their lives. Why because those are the most important areas in each of our lives and so we monitor them. Constant examination will qualify our children for quality growth under normal conditions.

So what are the important things to you that need to be examined? What is the things that should be monitored in your life? For the farmer it's his plants which he monitors daily for anything that may interrupt a normal growing procedure for the seeds that's been planted. The farmer knows the quality of his harvest will be determined on how attentive he is during the growing process of the seed. So the farmer checks the soil of the ground daily. If it hasn't been enough rain he knows to water the plants. If he see's that there are weeds he knows he needs to pull the weed. He knows that when he does plant the seeds that the seed have to be planted deep enough so the seeds will not be disturbed in anyway.

He also knows that there are other assorted things that he must do to ensure the health of his plants. Also again the farmer can not hope that the plants will come forth, he cannot think the plant is coming forth, he need to know that the plants will come forth. The farmer knows the harvest will come forth because he checked the conditions and continued to monitor the health of the plants.

The farmer is truly the example of a mother hen waiting for her chicks to grow to full maturity. He goes thru this process every year of his life as a farmer. He goes thru the planting and thru the waiting and then finally the harvest. This is the mindset that the people of God must have. We must have the mind set of planting. Taking in consideration the conditions in which we plant. We should plant in a spiritual environment that is conducive to growth such as planting a seed in faith.

We want to sow our seeds deeply in faith so our seeds cannot be disturbed by the enemy. We want to inspect our faith daily; we want to check our level of expectation as we wait for God to bring harvest in our life. When we have met the conditions that bring forth harvest, then we shall confidently know that our harvest will come forth. We don't have to think that our harvest will come forth; we don't have to say to ourselves that maybe our harvest will come. We will know that our harvest will come because our seed has been planted in the fertile ground of faith. So we can expect with great expectancy concerning our request from God. It is a great thing to see a process of God all the way thru. It's great to know God's moving and to witness his move to completion it is amazing and spiritually moving. If we plant right we can expect a great harvest without fail, in fact however we plant we shall bring forth harvest.

The key is how and what kind of condition will our harvest come forth. We all want a healthy harvest so we can reap the benefits of our labor. God wants us to enjoy our labor and because he wants us to enjoy our labor we wait in expectancy. We wait and know that God is a master farmer and knows how to bring forth a great and healthy harvest.

God has given us the equation for sowing and reaping, he has showed us the way to a vibrant harvest if we take heed to his instructions. Expectancy is truly a vital principle when it comes to receiving from the Lord. God honors you when you expect from him, he honors you when you trust him and put the outcome in his hand. He loves when you expect the best. So I say trust God always, always be in the realm of expectancy when dealing with God in everything you do. Expectancy brings on God best, not only will it bring on God's best it will bring the best out of you. Come on and give God some praise right now because we know and expect that the best is yet to come.

HE IS A WONDERFUL GOD, GREAT AND ALMIGHTY

JUST DO IT
CHAPTER SIX

I know you have heard of the slogan that has been so known since the days of Michael Jordan basketball career. The slogan JUST DO IT. It's really a simple slogan but it has so much meaning to it. How many of us have heard a simple phrase in our life but the rich jewels of wisdom that it contained was plentiful. Well the slogan JUST DO IT is one of those phrases that carry a wealth of wisdom. This slogan just seems to stick to your mind and spirit every time you hear it, especially when you hear it at the right time. In times when you are caught between two opinions, times when you have fear, times when you need strength to achieve something, hearing this slogan gives you motivation to move out.

This slogan almost seem like it should have been a verse in the bible because of its motivation factors. When you hear this slogan it sort of erases every excuse in your mind about deciding to tackle some task that you might have been procrastinating to do. It seems as thou as if it jogs the mind and the spirit. It urges you to go in spite of what you feel or what dilemma you may be in. The word of God says that faith comes by hearing and by hearing of the word of God. So hearing is what gets our faith to the point of accomplishment. We hear the word and the word produces the spiritual motivation to completion. So the slogan JUST DO IT is three words that spark movement, even in the most lethargic person or in the most notorious procrastinator. It is simply saying cut through all the red tape and see the goal and head for the goal and know that nothing can stop you and nothing will stop you. This awesome phrase instills in us a level of tenacity that will help us realize that we are much wiser and stronger than any obstacle that tries to stand in our way. Hearing this phrase seems to double our strength and courage. This phrase will give us the courage to make the necessary decisions we need to make in our lives, it will also help us see them thru. I know it is just a simple phrase and some of you might be saying why is he making such a big deal out of a phrase that comes from the world. The world has said great powerful things that contained great wisdom. Take the saying cleanliness is next to Godliness. In my experience when I'm clean physically, mentally and spiritually I feel this is when I am the closest to God. This is a worldly saying but very profound in wisdom.

The reason why I named this chapter JUSTDO IT its because this phrase explains what the children of God need to do. We need to forget about our excuses and fears which keep us from moving out in God. I just want to say that all the chapters in this book relates to each other concerning the process of accomplishing and receiving from God. I truly believe that except you take hold of this which I am revealing in this book you will not accomplish much in the kingdom of God.

I believe that these principals must be lived by if we desire to be effectual in God's kingdom. What good is to have the plan to greatness and never be great? We must take the principles of God to heart always. This chapter JUST DO IT is the cumulating sum of all that has been said in this book. This is our faith being mobile in the physical world. The bible says works without faith is dead. In the book of James the bible says that even the demons believe, hear and tremble when it comes to the authenticity of the power of God's word. You know its all well and good we have faith, but the question is do we have faith that is alive and moving.

The point is that our faith has to be alive and moving in the direction that the will of God is calling us to go. But we hesitate sometimes and procrastinate when it comes to using our faith as a moving power. Some of us have fear of the unknown, some are just plain scared to fail and so we never move out. But this is the most strategic attack the Devil imposes on the children of God, fear, and the fear of failure. But God did not give us the spirit to fear but he has given us a spirit of power, love and of a sound mind. The Saints knows nothing but victory in God. The Saints knows that God has already given us the victory and because we know we have the victory we can move out with confidence knowing nothing can stop us. Sure we'll be apprehensive at times and sure we are going to fear but this fear should not immobilize us to the point that we cannot accomplish the will of God. God knows that we are frail in this earthly tabernacle, he understand these earthly traits.

This is why Jesus is our Great Mediator in heaven, Jesus walked this earthly walk and can testify to the feelings and the traps of this world which in turn he is able to plead our cases to the father. But still even thou Jesus can testify to the feelings and traps of this world, he still testifies that you can do all things thru him because he will strengthen us to do so. God promises you that when you do get into this emotional realm we ought to know that Jesus has provided a way out which is our faith. It's our faith that's going to release us to our victory as we walk out the things of God. How do we walk them out? We walk out the things of God by receiving a word from him and immediately setting out to accomplish what we heard. One thing we should remember if God spoke it then there is nothing that can stop it from coming forth. God shows you the places he wants you to go, he shows you the people he wants you to communicate with.

So we must be faithful in walking if we are going to be successful. As we walk toward the places God called us to our faith grows because we sense the Holy Spirit walking with us. The more we walk the clearer we hear God voice telling us where to go. The closer we walk with God there's a greater intensity to accomplish God's word in our life. You know it's a beautiful thing to see the goal line it gives you a greater push to get there. Walking towards the goal by faith settles our mind about our outcome as we undertake the things that God has given us to do. We must always be moving towards accomplishing the will of God's in our lives. Thou we may move out with fear sometimes we yet still allow the word of God destroy the fear as we walk towards our goal. The goal is to walk by faith and not by sight.

What is some of the things that will keep us doing what God has given us to do?
Prayer
Fasting
Obedience
Confession

The words that I have just mention are weapons that the Saints of God should possess if they are to move on towards the goals that God has ordained them to accomplish. I'm not going to explain the weapons that the children of God possess but you can study these weapons and come to understand them so you may stay the course.

You can be sure that our weapons that I mention are more than enough to help us accomplish our goal. They are abundantly fortified with the power of God. We are blessed with weapons that keep the enemy at bay as we pursue the prize. The weapons of God make the enemy power ineffective when it comes to the Saints of God. When we know our weapons it frustrates the enemy. The enemy knows there is nothing he can do to stop the Saints when a Saint knows his weapons of warfare. When you know the weapons you can move on in complete confidence that nothing can harm you and nothing will harm you because the bible says so. Our weapons are spiritual but the Devil wants us to fight with natural weapons he knows natural weapons will never defeat him. If we can always remember that what we face is spiritual and not natural we will always stay on course and not be deceived and manipulated by the Devil.

He wants us to react in the natural when it comes to spiritual things, he want us to move in the natural because he knows that in the natural we will never be effective. In the natural we can't fight off the Devil as we go out to accomplish a thing. The weapons I mention will keep us going towards God and our goal. We have a spiritual enemy thou he uses the things in the natural to attack us at times. We must keep in mind at all times that every attack starts from the spiritual and not the natural. Spiritually we need to know that we can defeat the Devil in every way providing we understand that we must fight in the spirit.

We are fighting in the spirit when we use the spiritual weapons that God has equipped us with. This is why it is so important to understand the nature of the spirit and what power we hold when we understand that spiritually we have all power over the Devil. We fight with the word of God inside of us which is Jesus. We all know that when Jesus is inside, greater is he that is in us than he is in the world. We fight knowing that the promises of God will never come back void; we understand that his word will accomplish any and everything it has set out to do. We understand that God will give us according to his riches and glory if we allow him to be God and in turn wait on him.

Even when it comes to really hard things like sickness and mental illness we can be at ease knowing we are able in every situation to cast out these tough spiritual spirits. Jesus cast them out with no problems in the Gospels. Jesus spoke to many demons of sickness and infirmities and immediately they obeyed Jesus and came out of the body of the possessed victim. Our weapons provoke miracles when we use them. Our weapons when we use them change the spiritual atmosphere because we take authority over whatever is present. We demand authority because of the word that is in us. The word of God has authority over all it shall never fail. Before the word of God fail the universe will roll up into itself, eternity will become finite before God word fail. So be always assured that God's word shall do the necessary work.

Sickness is an area where the Devil wants us to really stay ignorant of spiritual authority. Ignorance of spiritual authority causes so many of God's children to perish by the millions. The Devil doesn't want us to come to understand that we can be healed spiritually by God. He wants us to think that a miracle is impossible when we get sick. He want us to think that when a terminal spirit of sickness come upon us like cancer we can't speak and take authority over this spirit and cast it out by the power of God. Immediately he wants us to think that we are going to die without the hope of God healing us. Many of us have known people that God has healed from cancer divinely we can testify to the fact. But it seems our immediate reaction to this sickness is fear, our faith seems to go right out of the window. We're overtaken even thou we have witnessed the fact that God has healed people we know with this same disease. We hear the report from the doctor and immediately we freak out and start thinking negative about the situation.

I know cancer is a truly a disease that no one would ever want to suffer from. It kills millions of people daily around the world. The very fear of this disease has the ability to mentally stress a person out to the point of not having symptoms of this disease to having symptoms. Our negative thoughts can easily bring about symptoms of this disease in our lives. The fear of hopelessness immediately takes over and we find ourselves in a spiritual pit immobilized by the unknown. Our negative thoughts take away our hope, it totally shipwrecks our faith and it releases us to the torment that we invoke on ourselves.

Many continue to suffer at this level because we don't believe God will or can heal us. This is the mindset that the enemy tries to use against God people. But we have scriptures that help battles the fiery darts of the enemy. When we are sick we can cry out what the book of Isaiah mentions. It says that Jesus was wounded for our transgression, he was bruised for our iniquities and the chastisement of our peace was upon him and by his stripes we are healed. When it comes to money, the bible says in Philippians that he shall supply our every need according to his riches and his glory. For loneliness the bible says that he will never leave or forsake us. Because we have defense against the attacks of the Devil he does not have a way to stop us. We don't allow him to come in and exploits our feelings. We come to know that if we allow him to exploits our feelings we will eventually allow our feelings to become an excuse to why we can't move out by faith and do what God has called us to.

He wants to exploit us in everyway possible, he want us to come up with excuses that will stop us from taking the territories that God has ordained us to take. He wants us to make excuses not to take the cities, he wants us to make excuses not to go in the drug infested neighborhoods and take the captives, he want us to make excuses not to go in the prisons and take territory, he wants us to make excuses not to go in the hospitals and heal the sick, he want us to make excuses not to be pastors, bishops, evangelists. Excuses will stop us from walking and God wants us to walk towards our victory and do what he called us to do right in the midst of the Devil. We that love God knows that God will take care of us in everyway. Again I use the scriptures in Mathew 6 the bible says that God supplies us with meat and drink for the body, and also raiment which is clothing for the body. He explains that he takes care of the birds in the air and then he goes on and says that he will do so much more for his children. When it comes to taking it by force, we can think about how in Genesis Abraham defeated the four evil kings with 318 men. We can think how in the book of Judges Gideon destroyed his enemy with just 300 men.

We can read how in Exodus how God used Moses to set the Israelites free. Even thou Moses were fearful at the beginning. All the great men and women of the bible had to move past excuses, they had to walk in faith to do what God called them to do. They knew they had to do the will of God and sure some of them gave their lives for the cause but the bible says again in Mathew: What if a man gain the whole world but loses his soul? We can live under our own power and by our own desires. We can seek wealth and make that our great desire for the reason we live. But this lifestyle will not heal the world nor will it get us to heaven.

Healing is the most effective thing that I know here on the earth. Healing entails making anew the sick, and there is much sickness and many categories of sickness in this world. Take a minute and I believe you can come up with about 50 different categories of sickness. But surely God has given us the power to defeat the enemy that comes up against us. The bible says that no weapons formed against us shall prosper. Sickness will not prosper because God's word is greater than any sickness. Romans: says in all these things we are overwhelming conquers. So there is no enemy that can stand against us. When we realize what power we have over the enemy we then understand that nothing can stop us from advancing. We walk determined to take those things by faith in which he has given us. It is he and his love that pushes us ever so closer into the territory we so feared. It is God that helps us along even thou we go timidly at times but yet we still go.

Sure this isn't an e*asy* life, at times it seems like the whole horde of hell is descending upon us at times. The fight to keep the Devil from infiltrating our lives can leave us weary in this old walk. Sometimes we can't see the forest for the trees. But something on the inside of us tells us just to walk toward God. The witness inside of us tells us that sooner or later everything is going to be alright. We tell ourselves that this trouble won't last forever and so we continue to walk with God. We come to know that it is not all about us, which sometimes we make it all about us.

Regardless of how spiritual we think we are we all get into that mold of thinking that everything is about us. Yes many battles we fight so we can continue in God's word, but the greatest battle will be against ourselves. We are surely our worst enemy in more ways than one. This is why we thank the Holy Spirit for revealing to us ourselves so we can ask God for deliverance from our spiritual flaws. Precious things the Devil has taken hold over because of our spiritual flaws as individuals. Our spiritual flaws and lukewarm attitude concerning the church as a whole have given room for the Devil to wreak havoc in our churches. The Devil secures his position daily as the church continues to go off track. He secures his position because we made the church a battle ground for Preachers and Laymen. We have made the church more about personal gain rather than worldly distribution. It seems as thou everything is pointing to me, myself, and I in the church these days. God is ever longing for the church to take its place in this dying world.

Just do it!!! We need fearless Saints like never before going forward without reservation, without fear, without doubt and apprehension. We surely need the boldness in God to deliver into our hands the things which God has assigned to us to take. We need the desperation of the Saints and the unending willingness to destroy the works of this evil Devil. We are wrestling with this Devil but we are wrestling in ineffective ways and this is why it is evident that the kingdom of darkness continues to expand itself in greater proportions.

Surely the Devil has surveyed the level of the church effectiveness and has reached the conclusion that he can take territory because of the breach in the covenant that we have made with God. We promised God to go on in our confessions. We promised to be faithful so God will be pleased with us. But sometimes I can say even in my own life I have fallen short and because I have fallen short I know that many of you has fallen very short of God's expectation as well. But how many can say from this day and at this very time we shall turn away from the things that keeps us from accomplishing the will of God. Can we make a declaration that we shall take the land, free the captives and give God all the glory for giving us the power to do so? We shall not give any more excuses of why we can't just do it.

This is truly an essential declaration that we make because we all need to go in the places we have neglected. What places have God told you to go in, what movements have God told you to begin by faith and you disregarded his plea. How have the Devil entangled himself in our walk that made us unmotivated in the work of God. What deception, what spell do he have you under, what level of fear that stops you from doing what you know God has called you to do. What blessing is he stopping you from receiving because of unbelief? We must be cleansed of these traits of unbelief and washed in the blood of the power in Jesus. We need to be cleansed of me, myself and I for the world's sake. We must step out as the warriors of God once again, who will get the job done if it's not you?

We have been called with this call to bring and compel men to God. If we are not on our job the Devil is going to keep compelling men to himself and hell is going to continue to enlarge itself with the souls of this world. But I say let's enlarge the kingdom of God with people of God, let us wait on God in patience so we may receive God's blessing upon our life. Let us stay encouraged enough to draw the sinners to the feet of Jesus. Let us do just that and not give it a second thought. We want to take and continue to take that which is of God and give blessings on to God so we bring him glory and honor. Surely we see the desperation of this dying world, the death of this world rings out like Sunday School church bells. God has given us the solution to heal the world but we continue to neglect the call. So I admonish you let us move past ourselves and fight the good fight. Let us run the race of endurance. Finally whatsoever God has given us to do, whatever he has showed us to take, whatever he has given us to wait for let us do these things in a new found fresh desperation. Let us bless God and in turn bless the world.

HE IS WORTHY!

SERVING WITH JOY
CHAPER SEVEN

As Saints of God there is a great sense of gratitude for God for saving us. There is a great sense of reverence and awe when we think of his awesomeness and his will to make us great. We think about how far God has brought us. We can do nothing but praise him and thank him from the bottom of our heart. We think about the wonderful deliverance that the Lord has bestowed upon us, we think about the love he has shown us when we didn't love ourselves so we praise him for it all. We know we should have been dead a long time ago. We think about how God manifested himself in our most turbulent times in our lives and changed us into new creatures.

2 Cor: 5-17 If any man be in Christ Jesus he is a new creature, behold old things has past away behold old things has become new. God has made us new creatures and changed our very nature. Because he has changed our nature we now conduct ourselves not like our old selves that loved sin and iniquity but rather we now love the things of God. The things of God have opened our eyes to a realm of peace which by we desire to live in and to live by. Real peace is a new state we didn't know exist. It was impossible to know that a level of peace existed on this level. We had to come to know God before we were able to enjoy peace on this level.

We are genuinely happy about our transformation of power we now experience. We are now able to live above the things that use to bind us up. We are undoubtedly happy that we are able to live and not find ourselves in gripping fear when it comes to our emotions. We finally see we don't have to be controlled by our emotions, but rather we can command our emotions to line up with God. We now understand that the power is not in how much we move but the power is in when God tells us to move and thus we move out. We come to understand this valuable lesson, a lesson which has freed us from useless works and unnecessary pain and suffering. How many know that allowing ourselves to engage in works that God hasn't called us to do can be exasperating when our labor doesn't come to fruition.

Our work didn't come to fruition because God did not call us to it. So from these experiences we have learned to wait on God leading. When we wait on God we can be sure that our harvest shall bring forth abundantly. How many has come to love when God invade our lives. We live and work for God to experience this in our lives. We have come addicted to the presence of God, those that serve him with a true desire. We have come to understand that we cannot live without his presence in our lives. We dare not allow ourselves to walk independently without him.

We know that we weren't much good when we lived a separate life void of God. The remembrance of this makes us shudder as we think about the dark places we have been blessed to come out of. So now we understand that we are going to live with God and by living with God we will never have to experience places like this again in our lives. How can I ever thank God for such wonderful exploits in my life? How can I ever give him enough thanks and praise? Do I ever think that I can praise him enough? Personally I don't think any of us has enough praise and thanks inside of us to bestow on God for the great things he has done in our lives. I think we would have to live a million lives before we can thank and praise him enough. Surely God has been good and extremely loving to consider us as one of his children. We are extremely thankful to be one of God chosen. I think about what the word of God says. It says that many have been called but few have been chosen. We ought to give God some praise right there.

We have been called as one of the chosen ones to enter into our final rest with God. To know that we are going to rest with our God will be the greatest experience we will ever have. Just my experience with him existing on the earth at this present time is astonishing to me. His presence is truly desired in our lives when we come to know him. When we have real experience with God we cannot forget him. God has brought us forth with his loving kindness even thou there were hard times, but we yet understand that all that we have gone thru has been meant for our good. So we look back and know that his loving kindness is what brought us thru. He could have let the gun go off; he could have allowed the unseen dangers in our lives destroy us.

But God fully had his hand on our lives even while we were yet still in our sins. He still took care of us he didn't allow the fatal blow to end our life. What if God never choose us? What if God never considered us? What if God never looked upon us and brought us out from under the sin that was killing us? What if he never removed the hurtful people who were stumbling blocks in our lives? Really what if God never took interest in us? I know for sure I wouldn't be this secure about my life at this present time. I wouldn't be as fearless and dedicated to life as I am right now. It is because of God and only God that we even think about our eternal rest. There are people slipping into eternity not knowing what awaits them but we do. We know what awaits us at our time of our death. We come to know that we will be with our savior in eternity.

John 3:16 For God so loved the world that he gave his only begotten son and whosoever believeth on his name shall not perish but have everlasting life. John explain that we shall have everlasting life with the father but those that haven't accepted Christ as their savior will not experience this setting. They will not experience the gold layered streets in heaven. The world doesn't understand that God has provided them away out from this tragic state. Christ have come in the world and died as an atonement for our sin, meaning he has paid the price for our sin. Christ paid the price for our sin which cleared the path to forgiveness and reconciliation to our God. Because Christ has done this we have eternal life. Eternal life is for those that has acknowledged of hrist death and resurrection and believe the very fact that Christ died for our salvation. So what more can us as Christians ask for when God has given us everything?

I know that we only see and experience these things in part right now, but when we shall see him we shall come to know the fullness of his glory. Aren't you happy that you are going to know the fullness of his glory, aren't you happy that in spite of what we experience here on earth it shall bring forth a reward when we come into his kingdom. Is he not awesome? Surely he desires nothing but great things for us. He desire great things because he is great. Great is he and he shall surely make us great if we give him the chance to do so. This is our confidence this is our experience in knowing God. He is never to be thought of someone that is too weak and fragile to do a thing. But we that are his children lift him up in praise and we worship him for his faithfulness to us. We know that there is no one more faithful than God. We know there is no one that cares more about us than God.

I know he will always be there when everyone else is gone. Its great learning to lean on the everlasting arm of God, we lean because God is big enough to bare it. He bares it because he told us to bring all our problems to him. Math: 11:28-30: Come unto me all ye that labor and are heavy laden, and I will give you rest. Take my yoke upon me and learn of me for I am meek and lowly in heart and ye shall find rest unto your souls, for my yoke is easy and my burden is light. We are blessed to hear someone say come and tell me your problem, come and give me your problems and I shall bring rest and peace upon you. God knows the state we're in when we carry around the weight of our problems alone. We are blessed to know that God knows how to manage everything he takes from us. He uses his awesome wisdom to relieve our hurts. God knows how to put us at rest.

He knows how to lay us down in the green pastures in which Psalms 23 talks about. The bible says that the Lord puts a new song in our heart. He does a new thing in our life, while he takes the old thing and make it the new thing. God is our master potter; he shall continue to work on us until we're molded into his image. He shall never be finished with us until the day of Jesus Christ coming. We all need to say that God is not finish with me yet. I don't care where we are in life right now we still need to declare that God still isn't finished with me yet. He still has so much more work to do on us. I don't care what level of sin you find yourself in at this point God still has a plan for you.

I don't care how old you are he isn't finished with you. I don't care how mean you are as a Christian right now he still isn't finished with you yet. I don't care who tries to stand in our way, nor do I care what others think about us my God isn't finished with us yet. He won't be finished until we see the face of Jesus and when we see him as he really is then we shall know that God has finally finished with us here on earth.1Thessolonians 4: 15-17. For this I say unto you by the word of the Lord, that we which are alive and remain unto the coming of the Lord shall not prevent them which are asleep. For the Lord himself shall descend from heaven with a shout with the voice of the archangel and with the trump of God and the dead in Christ shall rise first.

Then we which are alive and remain shall be caught up together with them in the clouds to meet the Lord in the air and so shall we ever be with the Lord. So when the Lord descends from heaven to call us home for all should know that our work is over. We should know that our labor is finished and our reward awaits us in the hands of the precious father. We will all go home from this tedious work we shall all have our rest a rest that will be well deserved. Can you see being caught in the air with our master the one who called us and made us great in the kingdom? It will be glorious to see the face of the one that delivered me from crack cocaine.

What a privilege to have this great God in our lives. I'm just so grateful deep in my heart for the things that he has done, he has changed me forever. I've been changed by God inwardly and outwardly which is truly a testament to his power. I will love and praise him forever for this mighty thing he has accomplished in my life. How can it not be praise inside of us for what God has done? I come to find out in life that there will always be something to praise God for. There should be praise for God for who he is and not always for what he will do for us. I know the horrific things that God has majestically delivered us from will always be the bedrock that keeps us believing in him. We should never let nothing deter us from his most gracious and loving spirit. We are blessed beyond our imagination, loved beyond thought and boundaries, and surely we have come to know that God will always be God in our lives.

As Christians we understand God didn't have to make a way for us but he did. I praise God for his love and care he has shown in my life time. We now know that he is all powerful and knows how to deliver us from overwhelming situations that tries to overtake us. We now know that we don't have to worry about the Devil overtaking us with his schemes and manipulation. We know now that we don't have to be apprehensive about his tactics of fear based scenarios that he presents to us. We have come to know that ultimately we have the victory in every case and every situation that may arise in our lives.

Because we know God and his prevailing power we have acquired confidence in our Lord. We have come to acquire confidence in his ability to keep us which in turn gave us joy, unspeakable joy in our lives. God gave us confidence in him when he gave us victory after victory over the things that use to utterly defeat us. Our victories brought smiles and joy in our life, a joy that we never experienced before. Let me tell you we should always know that the joy of the Lord is our strength. Godly joy will always be a weapon against the Devil and his schemes. Joy cancel out fear, hopelessness, depression and any other spirit that tries to invade the life of God's children. Our joy is such a great weapon this is why the Devil tries to steal it from us at every chance he gets. This is why we should meditate on Jesus and the word of God daily; we meditate so we can keep our joy.

We are God's children and his children have joy because of God. Before God came into our lives we were cornered into dark places and filled with desperation. But now we have been placed in the light so the whole world can see how God has called us out. We are joyful because we can now be a testimony to the world. We are joyful because we can now be a testimony to our families who desperately need proof of God's working in our lives. What will bring someone in the kingdom but the spirit of God and the joy of the Lord. Thank God that many of us have taken hold of this and made a stance to live joyful. The world right now really needs joy because trouble is everywhere.

When I take a close look at the world I can see that there is not too many places where joy live. There is much laughter going on but there is really no joy. People are laughing rather than crying out about their pain. They are hiding their feeling and presenting false laughter. Laughter is the defensive shield that most people use to deliver themselves. People are using so many useless devices; they are leaning on so many fallible things. Ultimately they become disappointed because the fallible things are not sufficient enough to keep them. The harsh reality of the situation is that they will continue in their tornado of pain and hurt without any real remedy. People of the world are killing each other because of the lack of joy. Marriages are dying because of the lack of joy. We that are Saints must continue to take on the task of being joyful in the Lord so we can reveal to the world a secure state of being in God. People need to know that joy still should be relevant and revealing even when situations is disastrous and constant.

We come to know that joy is not just an event but it is a state of being. The Lord doesn't give us temporarily fixes, he isn't a temporarily God. Everything God does for us is able to withstand any and everything that may occur in our lives. God gives us laughter but our laughter is derived from the state of joy. God understands that the Devil is a menace and a shrewd killer of the Saints; he also knows if we are going to withstand the Devil onslaught we need substance and deepness in spiritual strength.

He understands that through it all we must learn to stand with the weapons he has given us. And the greatest weapon that God has given us is our joy. So what God has called us to do there should be no fear to continue on the path in which he has ordained us to travel. As vision manifest itself we ought to know that nothing can derail us because of our joy. Our desire should catapult us into speaking and expecting relentlessly. When trouble does arise in our lives we should know that we have the joy of the Lord to strengthen us and the knowledge of God who takes seriously the welfare of his Saints. Surely God watches over us in the fire of our situations. God will walk us thru the fire so we won't be burned. He has never let us down or forsaken us in any way. We know our vision will take time to form and the wait sometimes will leave us discouraged. But we must understand that the Devil will attack your vision with everything he got. The Devil does not want to see the plan of God manifest in our lives. But we understand that this spiritual warfare is the path to our joy increasing.

Spiritual warfare will bring you to a more excellent standing in God. Spiritual warfare is designed to take you to greater levels of excellence. Warfare will allow you to become more proficient in your battles. When you learn to battle it will teach you to keep your cool as you go thru. There is nothing that the Devil hates more, a Saint that's going thru who maintains a cool demeanor. He cringes when he sees the Saints of God holding their ground without fear and apprehension. This reminds him that his time is at hand. He understands that there is a remnant of God that has no fear. He understands that this remnant is going to continue on with the plan of God. He knows that this remnant of God know the importance of encouraging themselves in this fight. He knows they have learned to fight in this spiritual war. But thou he knows this doesn't mean he isn't going to try to continue to trip us up.

We already know that he is relentless and will not stop taunting. But our joy keeps us going when the vision takes time to form, our purpose drives us on to completion. The spiritual intensity to see the will of God manifested in our lives is so overwhelming nothing can stop us in our tracks. The more the trouble the more we learn to adjust to what is going on. Acute understanding to spiritual warfare keeps us sharp in the fight. When we come to understand that everything is warfare we become much better soldiers. In our warfare we begin to record our victories over the Devil.

This helps us to understand that we can apply the same weapons for every attack the Devil wages against us. We come to know that faith in God and our spiritual weapons will always bring us out. We know that God is going to protect us and so we continue to state this fact. We are joyful because God is going to protect us as we continue to harvest from his plan in our life. This is something that must be remembered because without this truth our joy will be stolen by the Devil. This is a point that must be driven home for the sake of the kingdom and kingdom building. This is what everything is built upon in the kingdom of God. The point is that God is going to be with us in everything that we do.

Second Thessalonians 3:3
But the Lord is faithful, who shall establish you, and keep you from evil. Haven't we always found him to be faithful and willing? Hasn't he promised to keep us? Haven't we come to know that he won't let anything overtake us? God is faithful and because we know that God is faithful our desire is to be faithful to him. We want to do his will and give ourselves over to him completely so the works of God will be manifested thru us. God has done so much for us and because he has done so much we dream and envision pleasing God for the rest of our lives. We want others to feel the same way we feel about God and his awesome love.

I know I have spoken about this in the earlier pages. But I just want to reiterate that we are saved by the works of God. He uses us to work his will so salvation can be administered to others. This is why our salvation cannot be in a park position. We know salvation needs to be mobile in the kingdom of God. A salvation in a park position isn't beneficial to anyone. It's like having a car and we need to get to a destination but yet we keep the car in a park position. If the car stays in the park position we will never get to our desired destination. So what we naturally do is we get into the car and put the key in the ignition and start the car up and we drive to our destination. Our joy is the fuel that will keep our salvation out of the park position. Our joy drives us thru the path of suffering, down the streets of heartaches, off the freeway of pain, and finally to the rest stop of victory. Joy we come to know in a personal way because we see the great need for it in our lives. Our going forth in this walks reminds us that we need joy continually.

Every spiritual bump deepens our desire for it. Every victory entices us to know it in a greater way. How can the earth survive without sunlight? How can it survive without the four seasons? How can the earth survive without the protection of the second heaven? Everything survives from essential things which maintain its survival. Plants and trees need water and sunshine for their survival. The children of God have an essential need and that need is joy.

We need joy like the trees and plant need sunshine and rain. Without daily joy we will dry up and waste away. We will loose our effectiveness; we will become more of a hindrance than a help in the kingdom. Joy enables us to overrun the Devil and every stumbling block he sets before us. It allows us to see our path clearly because we learned how to see the big picture in everything we set out to do. Joy makes us look at the little things as being very little and makes the enormous things in our lives seem less intimidating. Of course enormous things like tragedies will get us down. But when the tragedies have been given over to God in due time we will begin to look at the big picture of Gods salvation plan in our lives. The big picture is that in our lives we come to know that the end results will always be greater than the immediate. In the end result we will always overcome the immediate pain and damage which is the promise that God has given to his children. There is a reward for all those that endure their suffering. The reward is fullness of joy in this world and the next.

Many just want to know the way out without actually physically dying. So can we be the ones that show them the way out so they can also live for God. Let's make a vow to be joyful before God so we can attract the lost and not be pushed away? The world needs us to be strong and powerful as we build in the kingdom. They need to see the desperation in our lives to bring forth purpose, and vision in our lives.

The world needs to know that for God we live and for God we shall die. Not that we are trying to convince them but that the spirit that moves us will draw them to the kingdom. We can withstand anything when we have joy. God has called us to be joyful people. In fact he has commanded us to be joyful. He knows that a joyful spirit is our greatest weapon against our enemies. He also knows that joy is our greatest attracting power to those that is lost. Again I say we that know joy knows how important it is to have it. People come to God everyday simply because they seen the joy of the Saints. There is a Christmas carol which I truly love and the name of it is called Joy to the world. In the song it states that Jesus has come in to the world and because he has come we now have joy.

So let joy rule in your heart as you work, let it bring songs of Zion in your spirit. Let us sing those joyful songs as we go thru our daily troubles. Let the world know why we sing. We sing because we are happy even when all hell is breaking loose. When all hell is breaking loose we are yet still full of joy. We that are saved have come to know that God is in control, he is faithful to bring us out every time. We also know that we have a home at the end of our lives with our God. So we stand ready to fight the good fight of faith. We stand in the fire of tribulation and endure with joy.

So that whosoever will come we will be able to say that this joy I have the world didn't give it to me but it comes from our Lord and Savior Jesus Christ.

JESUS OUR REDEEMER

CONCLUSION

We believe we are people of destiny, we know that our hope is in our Savior Jesus who saved us and granted us eternal life. So if our hope is in Christ well then we should believe what he tells us. In the word of God Christ tells us that if we believe we can tell the mountain to be ye removed and the mountain shall be cast into the sea. If we believe Jesus said greater things we will do. Only believing and applying what you believe by faith will manifest what you believe God for. Many of us pray but don't fully believe by faith and because we don't believe by faith our request isn't granted by God. When God doesn't answer our prayer or grant us the petition in the time we so desire we allow ourselves to get bitter and angry at God and we stop doing what we know is right by faith to do. Some of us return to the world when God doesn't answer us or give us according to how we feel God should bless us. But we don't have to return to the beggarly elements of the world. We just have to stretch our faith and believe God and know nothing is impossible.

Philippians 4:12
I can do all things through Christ who strengthen me.

This scripture is stating that there is nothing that I can't do when I depend on Christ. It clearly state that there is nothing that I can't do; there is nothing that I can't believe for. I can believe what I desire from God and receive it this is scriptural. God does not make promises that aren't genuine and true. What we need to do is just step out on faith. We have to make up our mind that we are going to believe God no matter what happens. We must understand that we have to have a pitbull spirit, a spirit that will hold on in faith even in the direst situations. We still must believe that our God shall strengthen us even in our storms of life. We have to believe that God wants the best for us; we also must know that the Devil will try everything in the book to stop us from receiving what God has for us. He doesn't want us to believe that God will not hold back any good thing from us. In spite of his demonic attacks on our mind and body he still hasn't the power to overtake us unless we allow him to. God will strengthen us in the time of trouble so we can go on believing him for the blessings we desire from him. Surely you have to believe this above everything us. We must know that God isn't a liar, his word is his bond and we can trust him to perform his word in our life without any suspicion.

We must know that he is God in our good times as well as our bad times. Yeah sure he doesn't come when we want him to, but we come to know that he is always on time. We can depend on him to come and do his work as a father in our lives. He isn't a God that treats his children as bastards he see his children as precious vessels and longs to bring joy in their lives. He cares for his children like precious vessels, precious vessels that he loves to interact with. He loves his relationship with us, he loves when we depend on him as he walks with us daily thru our lives. He loves it when we take all our problems to him and decide to leave them with him.

He loves making us into the warriors and disciples in which he called us to be. He loves it when he blesses you and in turn you bless others with his love. God will bless you by your faith, he will give abundantly and above all that you can ask or think. Your faith in God will always enhance your relationship with God. He is more than ready to bless us at any given time. God loves us so much that he creates the greatest ways to bless us. He blesses us in a way that you will know that only he could have blessed you. If we continue in God it will become undoubtedly clear that the handprint of God has been on our life since our birth.

So as long as we walk with God we will come to believe God, and everything that God said. I have come to know that whatsoever strength and earthly possessions I've obtained I know God supplied it out of his goodness. So we no longer believe that it has anything to do with us, but it has everything to do with God. We realize the more we stay out of the picture the more room we give God to work in our lives. God desire that we believe onto even greater things. He wants to show us what eyes haven't seen and ears haven't heard. This is why we can't think beyond God's giving capacity. I come to know that if you're ready to be shaped in the fire of God's Will then there is nothing you can't have.

You must be empowered and humbled to the point of receiving. God will not give you a million dollars and you can't manage five dollar. God isn't a God of confusion he is a God that does things decent and in order. He promises that if you do his will you will receive beyond measure. He is a God that gives us immeasurably; he gives liberally, and without respect of person. Our faith will determine what we shall receive from God. Your diligence and faithfulness will lay hold to everything that God has for you. Question is can I believe him to the point that I will follow him where ever he desires to take me and yet still maintain my faith. Mathews: 16:24-26: Then said Jesus unto his disciples if any man will come after me let him deny himself and take up his cross and follow me. For whosoever will save his life shall lose it, and whosoever will lose his life for my sake shall find it.

What if a man profits the whole world and lose his own soul? Or what shall a man give in exchange for his soul? In These scriptures Jesus is stating that if you desire life under the umbrella of God, we must deny the urges to allow ourselves to live under our own power. Without the grace and mercy of God many of us would have been dead long ago. Believe this in our own power we can not do the work that was done on the cross in which our Lord Jesus Christ bared for the world. We can not save ourselves from the punishment of hell under our own strength. Under our own strength we are fallible and weak.

Whatever we obtained here on earth has an expiration date. The blessings we obsess over can easily lead you from the presence of the Lord. We sometimes pursue that which has no eternal attributes. God did not call us to these earthly pursuits but he called us to his eternal rewards. The works of Christ surely has eternal value; his rewards will not waste away. Nothing can save us but our risen Savior which is our God Jesus Christ. We shall die and not have a free way to an eternity with God if we do not pursue him. What Jesus is making clear is that if you believe and follow him not only will you have eternal life but you will also have life and life in abundance here on earth. You can receive whatever you are hoping for as long as we let God bless it into our lives.

 We don't have to venture out on our own, on our own will be our death but in Christ its life. I rather have life than have death anytime. I rather lean on the everlasting arms of Jesus in this life. The song says that we are safe and secure from all alarms. I want to be safe and secure this is why I believe. This is why we all should believe that Jesus should always be our ultimate pursuit in this life. We should believe that thru him we are empowered to do any and everything thru him. We come to believe that there is nothing to fear when we continue in his presence. We understand that the commandment of God is that we continue believing God until the day of Jesus Christ return. This revelation will secure our place in heaven and will make our stay here on earth much more pleasurable.

For sure God is thinking about us in his quiet moments. We need not panic when we are not hearing from God at times. We need not panic when he hasn't delivered his promise to us. What should be such a part of us is knowing that he will deliver and give us abundantly more than we can ask or think. Humble yourself in the sight of the Lord and he shall lift you up. This is a verse in the bible that explains to us to humble ourselves before God. It explains that when we humble ourselves before him we are actually exalting him and in due time he shall exalt us. So let us not let the Devil see us sweat, let us show confidence and an unmovable belief in our Lord.

So purpose and all the other stages that I have explained in this book are inspired by the Holy Ghost. These are the principles, standards and procedures we must adhere to if we are going to do the things that God has called us to do. God reveals his standards and we must abide by them, if not we all know that a double minded man receives nothing from God. But we can all live truly on a greater plane of life; in fact we are call to live on a greater plane. God finds it not robbery to give us what we want, ask you shall receive, seek and you shall find, knock and the door shall be open unto you. So keep knocking, keep seeking, keep asking and most of all stay obedient. Obedience in God will surely cause your dream to come to pass. Remember stay with God and all that you ever wanted will be yours. So I say God bless you and may his blessing be multiplied on to you a hundred fold.

Let the joy of the Lord continue to strengthen you and may your hope and desire in God take you to levels of unspeakable joy.

God Bless You!!!

If you need me to preach or tell my testimony at your church, please write or call me.
Address: Carlton Jones
3811 Surf Ave Apt 1H N.Y. N.Y. 11224
Phone: 347-864-3265